What people are saying about …

CHARIS

"We often think that grace enters the Bible when Jesus appeared. However, Preston shows us that within the pages of the confusing, sometimes bizarre, and often war-filled pages of the Old Testament, there is heaps and heaps of grace. And the more we look, the more grace we see—grace that melts our hearts in worship of our God who shows His overwhelming, mind-blowing, over-the-top amazing grace from Eden to the New Jerusalem."

Dan Kimball, Leadership, Mission
and Teaching at Vintage Faith Church,
and author of *Adventures in Churchland*

"A book on grace with the power to liberate us from the weight of works and requirements and do-goodisms that have plagued Christians for far too long. Every page is bursting with freedom. Finally, a grace-filled book on grace!"

Jonathan Merritt, author of *Jesus
Is Better Than You Imagined*

"Preston Sprinkle writes a book on grace that is long overdue. Christians love to talk about grace and we name our churches Grace, but grace like God's is in desperately short supply. Sprinkle frees us to live in God's grace as Jesus embodied it. That kind of grace is unnerving, and for the most part, unprecedented in the Christianity most of us know. *Charis* is a must-read for every pastor, student, leader ... and anyone who has walked through the doors of a church and felt inadequate, judged, unworthy, or unspiritual. Preston brilliantly reminds us that God no longer sees you as the failed one, the messed up one. Because the kind of grace Sprinkle writes about changes it all, and God only sees you as precious and priceless. So much so that like a tattoo, your name is written on the hands of God. This is what makes *Charis* a game changer for all of us."

Palmer Chinchen, PhD, cultural artist and
author of *True Religion* and *The Barefoot Tribe*

CHARIS

GOD'S SCANDALOUS
GRACE FOR US

PRESTON SPRINKLE

David C Cook®
transforming lives together

CHARIS
Published by David C Cook
4050 Lee Vance View
Colorado Springs, CO 80918 U.S.A.

David C Cook Distribution Canada
55 Woodslee Avenue, Paris, Ontario, Canada N3L 3E5

David C Cook U.K., Kingsway Communications
Eastbourne, East Sussex BN23 6NT, England

The graphic circle C logo is a registered trademark of David C Cook.

The website addresses recommended throughout this book are offered as a
resource to you. These websites are not intended in any way to be or imply an
endorsement on the part of David C Cook, nor do we vouch for their content.

Unless otherwise noted, all Scripture quotations are taken from The Holy
Bible, English Standard Version® (ESV®), copyright © 2001 by Crossway, a
publishing ministry of Good News Publishers. Used by permission. All rights
reserved. Scripture quotations marked NASB are taken from the New American
Standard Bible®, Copyright © 1960, 1995 by The Lockman Foundation. Used
by permission. (www.Lockman.org.); MSG are taken from *THE MESSAGE*.
Copyright © by Eugene H. Peterson 1993, 2002. Used by permission of NavPress
Publishing Group; AMP are taken from the Amplified® Bible. Copyright © 1954,
1987 by The Lockman Foundation. Used by permission. (www.Lockman.
org.) The author has added italics to Scripture quotations for emphasis.

LCCN 2014937606
ISBN 978-0-7814-0788-5
eISBN 978-0-7814-1164-6

The Team: Alex Field, Karen Lee-Thorp, Nick Lee,
Kathy Mosier, Ingrid Beck, Karen Athen
Cover Design: Amy Konyndyk
Cover Photo: Veer Images

Printed in the United States of America
First Edition 2014

1 2 3 4 5 6 7 8 9 10

042814

For
Kaylea, Aubrey, Josie,
and Cody

CONTENTS

FOREWORD

BY TULLIAN TCHIVIDJIAN

The best definition for grace I know comes from Paul Zahl:

> Grace is love that seeks you out when you have noth-
> ing to give in return. Grace is love coming at you
> that has nothing to do with you. Grace is being loved
> when you are unlovable.... The cliché definition of
> grace is "unconditional love." It is a true cliché, for it
> is a good description of the thing.... Let's go a little
> further, though. Grace is a love that has nothing to
> do with you, the beloved. It has everything and only
> to do with the lover. Grace is irrational in the sense
> that it has nothing to do with weights and measures.
> It has nothing to do with my intrinsic qualities or
> so-called "gifts" (whatever they may be). It reflects a
> decision on the part of the giver, the one who loves,
> in relation to the receiver, the one who is loved, that

negates any qualifications the receiver may person-
ally hold…. Grace is *one-way love.*[1]

Grace doesn't make demands. It just gives. And from our vantage
point, it always gives to the wrong person. We see this over and over
again in the Gospels: Jesus is always giving to the wrong people—
prostitutes, tax collectors, half-breeds. The most extravagant sinners
of Jesus's day receive His most compassionate welcome. Grace is a
divine vulgarity that stands caution on its head. It refuses to play
it safe and lay it up. Grace is recklessly generous, uncomfortably
promiscuous. It doesn't use sticks, carrots, or time cards. It doesn't
keep score. As Robert Capon puts it, "Grace works without requir-
ing anything on our part. It's not expensive. It's not even cheap.
It's free."[2] It refuses to be controlled by our innate sense of fairness,
reciprocity, and evenhandedness. It defies logic. It has nothing to do
with earning, merit, or deservedness. It is opposed to what is owed. It
doesn't expect a return on investments. It is a liberating contradiction
between what we deserve and what we get. Grace is unconditional
acceptance given to an undeserving person by an unobligated giver.
It is one-way love.

Think about it in your own life for a moment. Odds are you
have caught a glimpse of one-way love at some point, and it made all
the difference. Someone let you off the hook when you least expected
or deserved it. A friend suspended judgment at a key moment. Your
father was lenient when you wrecked his car. Your teacher gave you an
extension, even though she knew you had been procrastinating. You
said something insensitive to your spouse, and instead of retaliating,
she kept quiet and somehow didn't hold it against you the next day.

truest truth in the entire universe. God loves us independently of what we may or may not bring to the table. There are no strings attached! No ifs, ands, or buts. No qualifiers or conditions. No need for balance. Grace is the most dangerous, expectation-wrecking, smile-creating, counterintuitive reality there is.

Grace is a bit like a roller coaster; it makes us scream in terror and laugh uncontrollably at the same time. But there aren't any harnesses on this ride. We are not in the driver's seat, and we did not design the twists and turns. We just get on board. We laugh as the binding law of gravity is suspended, and we scream because it looks like we're going to hurtle off into space. Grace brings us back into contact with the children we once were (and still are)—children who loved to ride roller coasters, to smile and yell and throw our hands up in the air. Grace, in other words, is terrifyingly fun, and like any ride worth standing in line for, it is worth coming back to again and again. In fact, God's one-way love may be the only ride that never gets old, the only ride we thankfully never outgrow. A source of inexhaustible hope and joy for an exhausted world.

Thank you, Preston, for writing a "no buts or brakes" book on grace. I can only imagine what the church would look like if more books like this were published.

PREFACE

Seriously? Another book on grace?

Trust me, this one will be different. I promise you.

This book stems from half a dozen years of teaching the Old Testament in a college setting. You might think this would produce a book about judgment, perhaps a book on hell, but no way. The Old Testament is all about grace. I tell my students that the reason we don't offer a course on grace is because we already offer several courses on the Old Testament. A class on grace would be redundant, superfluous, a swift kick to an already dead horse.

The Old Testament is a kaleidoscope of grace. And this book will admire its beauty. Genesis, Exodus, even Judges and Kings—they're all greedy to be read by tired Christians seeking rest. Isaiah, Ezekiel, Hosea—all singularly fixated upon God's stubborn grace. The Old Testament is one thick, adventurous narrative of God's reckless love toward unlovable people. Grace. *Charis.*

But we're getting ahead of ourselves. Without giving too much away, let me give a couple of warnings.

First, grace is a dangerous topic. We often want to domesticate it, calm it down, stuff it into a blue blazer and a pair of khakis. But biblical grace—or *charis*, as you'll see—doesn't like to settle down. It doesn't drive a minivan and it sometimes misses church. To prove this, we're going to venture on a journey across the land of Israel, and I'm not bringing a pacifier. If you need to scream, I'll roll down the window. If you want to get off in the next town, sorry, doors are locked. Grace is a dangerous topic because the Bible is a dangerous book. It wrecks people, it offends people, and it's tough to read from the suburbs. If you're under eighteen, you might want to find another book on grace. There are plenty out there.

Second, I'm not going to thoroughly explain how obedience fits in with grace. That is, not until the epilogue. In my experience, there are way too many "yes, grace, but …" qualifications to this risky truth, and they usually end up offending grace and celebrating our response to God. The epilogue will talk about our response to God. But the rest of the book will revel in God's response to us. I guess you could say I'm emphasizing only one side of the coin. Perhaps. But let's study that side, admiring its details and adoring its beauty. We often flip the coin around too quickly.

Several people have shaped my understanding of grace, and their fingerprints are all over the following pages.

My view of grace was significantly reconfigured by listening to sermons by Tullian Tchividjian, whom I've yet to meet. I've tried to stay clear of simply repeating what he's said, and if I do repeat, I've tried to give him credit. Pastor Tullian: I hope that if there still remains an uncited "Tullianism," it will give you honor. I hope this book will further substantiate much of your own passion for grace.

I should also note that in the initial stage of writing this book I caught a glimpse of Andy Stanley's book on grace and noticed that he, too, looks at the Old Testament. After thumbing through his book for a few minutes, I could see that he talks about some of the same passages that I do. So I quickly put his book down and didn't look at it again. Why? Because if Andy and I have made the same points or talk about the same passages, I can say that we found such pearls of grace independently. But, if we look at different Old Testament passages, then all the more evidence that grace is everywhere in the first half of the Bible. From what I've heard, my book is still quite different from Andy's.

I also thank my good friend and colleague Mark Beuving, who combed through every word of this book, as he's done with every book I've written. You should write your own book, Mark. Oh wait, you have!

Thanks to Alex Field and the crew at David C Cook for investing in me as a writer and enthusiastically accepting my proposal for this book. Thanks for not saying, "Seriously? Another book on grace?"

Thanks to my wife, Christine, for being my biggest fan. I couldn't write another book without you in my life. If loving someone despite his or her faults is grace, then your cup runneth over. Of grace … not faults. Did I get that right? I love you, babe.

And my kids: Kaylea, Aubrey, Josie, and Cody.

"Daddy, are you done with your book yet so we can go celebrate?"

"Yes, kids, I'm done. Let's head to Chili's."

Whenever I doubt God's grace in my life, I've got four invincible pieces of evidence to the contrary. Your laughs, your smiles, your energy, even your cries bring joy to my life. Sorry for smiling when you cry. You're just so darn cute when your bottom lip curls down to your chin. I love you all. And I dedicate this book to my four little monkeys.

A prayer:

Jesus, may these words capture a glimpse of Your boundless grace. Peel back our eyes and rip open our chests. Let us see and experience, know and cherish Your stubborn delight in undelightful people. If this book doesn't honor You, then please cause it not to sell. Amen.

1

CHARIS

JESUS LOVES CANNIBALS

God's scandalous grace invaded Portage, Wisconsin, with unwelcomed splendor in April 1994. It sailed past several churches and seminaries and targeted a criminal serving multiple life sentences in the Columbia Correctional Institution. It's not uncommon for thieves and murderers in prison to encounter God's grace, but this day was different. The villain who attracted God's love was a man who had killed, had sex with, dismembered, and eaten portions of (in that order) seventeen young men. Reviled as the epitome of human depravity—is *human* a fitting term?—Jeffrey Dahmer turned heads and stomachs with his imaginative acts of necrophilia and cannibalism.

His vile behavior elicited a nauseating response when it hit the news in the early '90s. How could this happen? America, a country that has a long leash on immorality, was stunned with disbelief.

But what happened in April 1994 was even more shocking than Dahmer's depravity. While in prison, Jeffrey Dahmer gave a television interview and mentioned in passing that he wished he could find some inner peace. A Christian woman named Mary Mott saw the interview and thought, *I know where you can find inner peace.* So she mailed several Bible studies to Dahmer. After receiving them, Dahmer immediately read them all and wrote Mary Mott back, asking for more. So she sent more. Shortly after, Mott contacted Roy Ratcliff, a minister who lived near the prison, and asked him to visit Dahmer to share the gospel with him. Ratcliff nervously agreed. He visited Dahmer, told him the good news about Jesus, answered some questions, studied the Bible with him, and eventually saw God's grace flood Dahmer's dark soul with life. Dahmer accepted Jesus as Savior and King—a deranged cannibal rearranged by grace.

Dahmer's bloodstained hands were washed clean with the blood of the Lamb. All the acts of murder, pedophilia, necrophilia, and cannibalism were thrust down to the bottom of the sea—no longer to have a voice in God's courtroom. Seven months later, Dahmer was killed by an inmate with a broomstick. And now, as far as we know, he's still celebrating his redemption with Jesus in heaven.

Grace, however, was unwelcome when it invaded Portage.

Many people were cynical, doubtful, even angry—like the Old Testament prophet Jonah—over Dahmer's "religious experience" in prison. Roy Ratcliff recalls with discouragement that many people he talked to doubted Dahmer's conversion.[1] And most of these doubters were Christians. "They ask if Jeff was truly sincere in his desire for baptism and in his Christian life. My answer is always the same: Yes, I am convinced he was sincere." Ratcliff is grieved. "Why question the sincerity of another person's faith?" If a person confesses Christ and yet fails to demonstrate any evidence that the confession was genuine, then there's room to doubt. But the cynicism lobbed at Dahmer's conversion did not focus on his postconversion life—whether there was evidence of faith—but the evil he committed *before* he came to Christ. "Jeff was judged not by his faith, but by his crimes."

According to Ratcliff, these Christian cynics believed that some crimes are too vile, too twisted, too unspeakable to be forgiven. We believe in grace. But we've got to draw the line somewhere. We've got to put a leash on grace before it runs free and breaks out of our gated community.

UNLEASHED

But grace has no leash. It's untamed, unbound, and runs wild and free. Was Dahmer's conversion genuine? If we go on evidence rather than skin-deep religiosity, then yes. But the church's response to Dahmer's conversion is telling. The doubt hurled at Dahmer's conversion gives off the foul odor of spoiled grace that's been sitting in church too long. Many Christians believe that rebels like Dahmer are unworthy of the fatted calf; they're appalled at the thought of our Father running after them. We've got to have some sort of balance— grace *and* justice. We need to keep grace under control. When it snaps our leash and runs loose, we get nervous.[2]

In many ways, the word *grace* has lost its stunning beauty, and perhaps through overuse, it's become just another Christianese buzzword. We use the word *grace* in flat ways. My students ask for "grace" when they turn in assignments late. "Come on, Professor. *Give me grace*." But divine grace is more than leniency, more than allowing exceptions to a rule.

Others say that grace means "unconditional acceptance." God accepts people even though they have not met His standard. This is true. Sort of. But it's still a decaffeinated definition. It fails to capture the divine aggression that invigorates grace and causes it to lurch upon the unworthy.

Grace is more than just leniency and unconditional acceptance. Divine grace is God's relentless and loving pursuit of His enemies, who are unthankful, unworthy, and unlovable. Grace is not just God's ability to save sinners, but *God's stubborn delight in His enemies*—yes, even the creepy ones. Grace means that despite our filth, despite the sewage running through our veins, despite our odd addiction to food, drink, sex, porn, pride, self, money, comfort, and success, God desires to transform us into real ingredients of divine happiness.[3]

Grace is God's aggressive pursuit of, and stubborn delight in, freakishly foul people. And since we all stood or stand guilty in God's courtroom—homeschooling moms, porn stars, Awana champions, and suicide bombers—we all urgently need the same stuff that rearranged Dahmer's soul. We all need grace.

CHARIS

We demean grace by reducing it to another Christianese buzzword. The original Greek word for grace is *charis* (with a hard "ch," like *karis*). *Charis* was not invented by Christians. *Charis* didn't originate with Jesus, Peter, or Paul. The word *charis*, in fact, was used widely in the ancient world where Jesus grew up. When Jesus walked through Palestine talking about God's *charis*, His hearers knew what the word meant. When Paul traversed the Mediterranean world heralding a message of *charis*, he would have been readily understood by anyone who spoke Greek. If Paul talked about *charis* in the marketplace, the vendors would have understood him. If he got into a debate with Greek philosophers, they, too, would have grasped the meaning of *charis*.

That's because *charis* simply means "gift." When we say "gift," the ancients would have said "*charis*." It means the same thing.

Rich people in the ancient world often gave *charises*, or gifts, to other people. They would donate *charises* to their hometown: a fountain in the city square, a statue of Zeus next to the courthouse. They would give a *charis* to someone in need of food or shelter. The wealthy were eager to give gifts to people. Why? Because the ability to give a *charis* showed (or showed *off*) that they had the means to give.

So Christians weren't the first people to talk about grace. But Christians revolutionized what *charis* meant, and here's why.

When rich people gave a *charis* to this person and a *charis* to that person—"here's a shekel to buy some food"—they didn't give it indiscriminately. The ancients gave *charises* only to those who *were worthy to receive it*. *Charis* was given to people who were worthy of *charis*: those who had a high status or who were morally upright, intellectually astute, or physically impressive. After all, we wouldn't want to squander our *charis* on some bum in the gutter who's unworthy of our gift. A rich person wouldn't waste *charises* on outcasts, the unappreciative, or thugs who had nothing to offer in return.

But Jesus did.

Jesus and His followers gutted the word *charis* and infused it with fresh meaning, with life-giving power. Jesus did more than give *charis* to the unworthy dregs of society. He made it His mission to seek them out. "The Son of Man came to seek and to save the lost" (Luke 19:10). He didn't just give *charis* to the beggars who crossed His path. Jesus hunted them down and showered them with gifts. The same Jesus who overturned tables in the temple overturned the social norms for dispensing *charis*. Naturally, Jesus would be especially drawn to cannibalistic fornicators with a sick attraction to dead people.

This is why Jesus was attracted to Paul. The apostle Paul didn't eat people, but he did try to kill several churchgoers, which made him a prime candidate for *charis* (1 Cor. 15:9–10). Targeted, hunted, and conquered by *charis*, Paul devoted his life to proclaim the message of the same leashless *charis* that he once found toxic. Sure, the ancients understood some of what Paul was saying: the gospel of *charis*, the good news about a gift given to those worthy of gifts. But Paul picked up where Jesus left off and infused this well-known term with the same unwelcomed splendor that rattled the prison cells of Wisconsin.

Our word *grace* has been overused and abused. It has lost its luster, its richness, its … *charis*. Perhaps through overuse, *grace* has become another nice term dumped into our worn-out bag of Christian lingo. We say grace before meals, include grace in gospel presentations, and slap the word *grace* on the names of churches. But if we never hug a harlot, befriend a beggar, or forgive our enemy seventy times seven, then we confess grace with our lips but mock it with our lives. First Church of Grace or Grace Fellowship or Grace Community—or whatever—should be an otherworldly safe haven where enemies are loved and porn stars are forgiven. That's *charis*.

Grace in the Old Testament?

God dipped His feather in *charis* when He penned the New Testament. Jesus hung out with harlots and drunkards, and He touched quite a few lepers during His short ministry on earth. Paul, too, could hardly talk about Jesus without clothing his message with a fresh understanding of *charis*. But such harlot-embracing, cannibal-forgiving grace is not just a New Testament thing. It's splashed across the Old Testament as well. This is why I want to admire grace through the lens of the Old Testament—that dusty, confusing, largely unread section that makes up two-thirds of our Bibles.

The Old Testament is all about grace. You can't understand grace apart from the Old Testament, and you can't understand the Old Testament without understanding grace. If you read the Old Testament and aren't kindled and confronted by the scandal of grace, then you need to go back and read it again. You missed it. If you see only wrath and judgment, then you've missed the best part, the main plot, the primary message. Grace is the spine that holds the whole thing together. Look at any story, any chapter, and you'll find a story of God's relentless pursuit of His rebellious children. Take grace out of the Old Testament, and, like pulling a thread from a sweater, the whole thing will come undone. Every character, every event, every single page from the Old Testament bleeds grace.

If you've read the Old Testament and didn't see much grace, don't worry. This is common. That's why I've written this book: to help us see the grace that's there. The reason we typically miss it is because we've been trained to read the Bible, especially the Old Testament, *morally*. That is, we generally look to the Old Testament as a showcase of moral examples to live by. We need to be like

Abraham, live like Jacob, and be a leader like Moses, Joshua, or David. We should fight like Samson, flee like Joseph, and stand up for God like Esther.

Is there a problem with this?

Yes. There's a huge problem with this. In fact, there are two huge problems with this.

First, this moral approach puts the emphasis on people rather than on the main subject, the primary character—God. God is the focus of every story in the Old Testament. Human characters play a role, but it's a supporting role and never the main part. The Old Testament—the whole Bible, really—is fundamentally a story about God, not humankind.

Second, most of the characters of the Old Testament are not good examples to follow. Abraham was a liar, Jacob was a cheater, Moses was a tongue-tied murderer, Esther broke more commandments than she kept and never even mentioned God, and Samson was a self-centered, vengeful porn star enslaved to lust and bloodshed. So if we follow our Old Testament "heroes" as Scripture presents them, we could end up in prison.

Instead of reading the Bible *morally*, we should read it *theologically*. This doesn't mean that there aren't some moral examples to follow. Yes, by all means, flee like Joseph. Nor does it mean hunting for verses that support our favorite theological doctrine. Rather, reading the Bible *theologically* means that we look first and foremost at what the passage teaches us about God. What is God doing? How is God revealing Himself? How is God going to overcome our sin, keep His promises, and reestablish the Eden-like relationship He created us for?

The Old Testament is all about grace, and it forms the rich soil from which Jesus's gospel of *charis* blossoms. To understand Jesus, we *must* soak ourselves in Israel's story of grace. That's why we'll end our adventure in this book by looking at the birth, life, and death of Jesus. Jesus is not just the beginning of the New Testament but also the fitting climax of the Old.

YOU CAN'T MAKE GOD LOVE YOU

There are many Christians in the church trying to make God love them. They spend their lives doing, serving, witnessing, fasting, judging, performing, and feeling the unbearable weight of condemnation when they fail at these things. They are *charis*-less Christians who atone for their sin by grinding out good works from a checklist. Such was the life of my friend Brad Sarian.

Brad was, in his own words, a modern-day Pharisee. He grew up in the church, read the Bible, prayed every day, shunned the very appearance of evil, and had near-perfect church attendance. When his Christian schoolteacher asked the class on Monday how many went to church, Brad shot up his hand like clockwork. "Yes, ma'am, I went to church *and* Sunday school."

Brad was a model kid. He never cussed, drank, smoked, or watched R movies, and he never looked at porn (well, almost never). He was not only a good, moral kid but also a gifted leader and an impressive preacher. By his early teens, Brad was teaching regularly in Sunday school, and by the time he was eighteen, he was the regular preacher for a vibrant junior high ministry at a megachurch in

Los Angeles. "As for the law," Brad told me, "I was blameless. I served the poor, discipled believers, and went on mission trips. And I *never* missed my devotions."

But there's one thing Brad missed growing up. According to his own admission, he never understood grace. "Oh sure, I could give you a textbook definition of what grace meant, but I thought grace didn't apply to me any longer." Brad thought of grace as a purely "past thing," something he needed when he first got saved. "Grace was what I needed for God to get me in the door to discipleship, Bible reading, and mission trips, but it carried no ongoing significance."

Brad's testimony is typical. He tells me that *every one of his friends at church* growing up had the same view of Christianity. Grace—and therefore the gospel—didn't carry any ongoing importance in their faith. Incidentally, 68 percent of born-again Christians in America believe that the saying "God helps those who help themselves" is a verse in the Bible—somewhere, perhaps, toward the end of 3 Kings. Not only is this phrase nowhere in the Bible, but the very idea is offensive to the biblical gospel. The good news isn't "God helps those who help themselves"; the good news is "You're wicked, your life's a mess, and only God can fix it." God helps those who realize that they *can't* help themselves.

"God seemed very distant during those years," Brad said. "He was like a distant father who would raise an eyebrow and spank me when I messed up but who didn't take a real interest in me as a person. When I messed up, I thought God was mad at me. So to please Him again, I would counter my sin with more good deeds. If I looked at porn, I would just memorize a verse that evening (or a chapter if I watched a lot of porn), and my sin would be covered."

2

CREATOR

TRANSCENDENCE

Genesis 1–2 explodes out of the gate with an awe-inspiring account of creation. God fashions the sky, forges the earth, forms Adam and Eve, and breathes cosmic firestorms into existence. Both chapters ripple with action and drip with intimacy. Most of all, Genesis 1–2 pulls back the curtain and reveals the main subject of the Bible. These chapters are fundamentally about God.

God is preeminent. God is ultimate. God is the main subject of Genesis 1–2 because God is the main subject of the entire Bible. I love how Rick Warren began his bestselling book *The Purpose Driven Life*. "It's not about you," Rick said. "It all starts with God."[1] And Moses, the author of Genesis, agrees. Genesis 1–2 is all about God: His character, His power, His majesty—*His grace*. Humans are swept up into the story of God. But the story is *His* story.

So what does Genesis 1–2 teach us about God? We'll begin with Genesis 1.

Every word in Genesis 1 magnifies the transcendence of God. The word *transcendence* means surpassing, beyond comprehension, or to exceed usual limits. It insists that God is not part of this creation but sovereign over it. He's without peer or competitor, and

He alone has the right and power to rule over creation as He sees fit. This is the God revealed in the opening chapter of the Bible. When He says, "Jump," planets leap into orbit. They don't ask, "How high?"

God whispers and stars explode into existence. God speaks, and massive balls of fire two hundred times the size of the earth suddenly exist.

There are over one hundred billion stars in each of the one hundred billion galaxies in the universe. That's around one sextillion stars, which is a number we get if we write out ten with twenty-one zeros behind it. There are 10,000,000,000,000,000,000,000 stars in the universe, each one spoken into existence by an all-powerful Creator. If we get too close to one of these stars—like ninety-two million miles away, the distance between the earth and the sun— and stare at it for more than five seconds, it'll fry our eyes. If there is an intelligent designer behind creation, then He must possess power beyond all comprehension.

"Lift up your eyes on high," shouted Isaiah, "and see: who created these [stars]? He who brings out their host by number, calling them all by name, by the greatness of his might, and because he is strong in power not one is missing" (Isa. 40:26). David wondered, "When I look at your heavens, the work of your fingers, the moon and the stars, which you have set in place, *what is man that you are mindful of him*?" (Ps. 8:3–4).

God is *transcendent*. He alone commands, speaks, blesses, declares, creates, forms, and hurls the universe into its divinely determined place. God creates this. God forms that. God puts this here. God tells that to go there. God whispers and creation stands at attention. Nothing just happens. Nothing is a struggle. Nothing is mundane. Everything is sacred.

So where does grace fit in?

Grace is everywhere in the creation account. It's in the rocks; it's in the trees; it's in the sky and under the sea. Grace is the *gift* of creation given to humanity.

God gave us creation. He made a cosmic playground and then told us to play.

CRACKED MIRRORS

After God showcases His transcendent power by speaking one hundred billion galaxies into existence, He says that the crown of His creation—the most majestic display of beauty and wisdom and power—is you.

> So God created man in his own image,
>   in the image of God he created him;
>   male and female he created them.
>
> And God blessed them. And God said to them, "Be
> fruitful and multiply and fill the earth and subdue
> it, and have dominion over the fish of the sea and
> over the birds of the heavens and over every living
> thing that moves on the earth." (Gen. 1:27–28)

You and I reflect God. When we look at people, or when they look at us, we see a reflection of the God of Genesis 1. We are created in His image. And because of that, our mission is to rule over God's earth and to be fruitful and fill it.

Have lots of sex and rule the world. If that's not grace, I don't know what is.

But what does the "image of God" mean? In what way do we reflect God? Above all, the image of God means that we have an exalted status above everything else in creation. We bear God's image not just by what we do—think, feel, imagine, relate—but simply by who we are. A quadriplegic two-year-old with Down syndrome possesses the image of God and *therefore* has infinite worth and value in the eyes of God, not because of what she does, but because of whom she reflects. Every human, every single one, bears the glorious image of the transcendent Creator.

Rich, poor, successful, homeless, healthy, disabled, black, white, brown, young, old, famous, abused, abusive, pervert, or priest—whoever you are and whatever you have or have not accomplished—*if you are human*, then you are cherished and prized and honored and enjoyed as the pinnacle of creation by a Creator who bleeds *charis*. If you're reading, listening to, or following the braille dots of this book, you are infinitely more majestic and beautiful than the glimmering peaks of Mount Everest, the soothing turquoise waters of the Caribbean, the commanding cliffs of Yosemite, or the well-titled Grand Canyon, which God carved out of Arizona.

God wants you to take pleasure in His earth, enjoy the people in your life, and rule over His creation. Ours is a giving God, and He longs for us to receive His *charis* with gratitude and delight.

And there's more.

GRACE IN THE GARDEN

If Genesis 1 emphasizes the *transcendence* of God, then Genesis 2 (specifically, 2:4–25) highlights the *intimacy* of God.

Transcendence and intimacy. We need both.

The two chapters reveal different aspects of God's character. God is far beyond us (Gen. 1), yet very near (Gen. 2). God is our King (Gen. 1), but also our Friend (Gen. 2). God is infinitely powerful (Gen. 1), yet intimately personal (Gen. 2). Genesis 1 shows off God's raw power. Genesis 2 showcases God's earthy affection. Here's how.

First, notice the different names for God in Genesis 1–2. Throughout Genesis 1, the English word "God" translates the Hebrew term *Elohim*. Thirty-five times, in fact, Moses writes the term *Elohim* to describe God, and he doesn't use any other term, such as the Almighty, the Holy One, or the Lord of Hosts.

But something changes in Genesis 2. Beginning in 2:4, Moses consistently writes "the LORD God," or *Yahweh Elohim* in Hebrew. Moses never just says *Elohim* in Genesis 2. He always says *Yahweh Elohim*.

Elohim is a generic term for God. Other ancient religions would have used the same term (or just *El*) to refer to their god. *Elohim* simply refers to a deity and emphasizes his (or her) power. And so it's fitting for Moses to use *Elohim* to refer to God in Genesis 1 when he wants to emphasize God's transcendence and power.

But *Yahweh* is God's personal name. My name is Preston, your name may be Joey, Sadie, or Mattie, and God's name is *Yahweh*. Now, in the ancient world, revealing your name to somebody was a sign of intimacy. While the title *Elohim* simply means that God is powerful, revealing His personal name *Yahweh* means that this powerful God also desires a relationship.

To show that our transcendent God gives the *charis* of intimacy, Moses describes Him as *Yahweh Elohim* throughout Genesis 2.

DIVINE MUD PIES

But God's intimacy is revealed in more than just His name. Look at the way God acts in Genesis 2. In Genesis 1, God hurls the universe into existence: sun, moon, stars, galaxies, mountains, and seas. But in Genesis 2, we find God playing in the dirt.

> Then the LORD God formed the man of dust from the ground and breathed into his nostrils the breath of life, and the man became a living creature. (Gen. 2:7)

God gets His hands in the soil and intimately forms man from the dirt. The word *formed* conveys the idea of "an artistic, inventive action that requires skill and planning."[2] It refers to an artist pouring out his ingenuity into an intricate work of art. A sculptor "forms" rock into a masterpiece; a potter "forms" clay into a work of art. And God steps down into His creation to show off the greatest display of His power, wisdom, and ingenuity. He fashions you.

God then takes this lifeless masterpiece and "breathe[s] into his nostrils the breath of life, and the man [becomes] a living creature" (Gen. 2:7). God takes Adam by the face and puffs divine breath into his lungs. He desires to be face-to-face with Adam. He touches and handles and carves and molds. And when Adam's hips and hair, fingers and face are just right—exactly how God wants them—He gifts him with the divine breath of life. When Adam opens his eyes and sucks in the sweet air, he finds himself in the presence of a God ecstatic over His greatest work of art.

The account of creation in Genesis 2 drips with intimacy. The God who creates (Gen. 1) also forms (Gen. 2). The God who manages stars (Gen. 1) mingles with humans (Gen. 2). But the most striking description of God's intimacy comes in Genesis 2:19:

> Now out of the ground the LORD God had formed
> every beast of the field and every bird of the heavens
> and brought them to the man to see what he would
> call them. And whatever the man called every living
> creature, that was its name.

This is one of those verses that you read a thousand times before it stands out. It seems like just another mundane detail, but stop for a second to imagine the scene. God forms all the animals and then brings them to Adam *to see what he would call them.* Does that seem odd to you? The God who commands the sun, moon, and stars into existence and gives them all names (a demonstration of authority) now lets Adam have a try.

"Go on, Adam, you have a turn! Why don't you name all the animals, and I'll sit over here and wait to see what you will call them."

How did that play out? I wish I could have been a fly on the Tree of Life to see Genesis 2:19 unfold. It must have been comical. God plops a small purring animal at Adam's feet and then steps back in anticipation to see what Adam will name it.

"How about … dog?" Adam says unconfidently.

"I don't know," God says. "We can go with dog if you want, but it's just not sitting right with Me."

Adam ponders. "How about … cat? Yes, c-a-t. What do you think about cat?"

"Cat!" God enthusiastically exclaims. "I love the name *cat*! I think we should go with that name, *if you want*."

God then brings a large gray animal with a long nose.

"How about … elephant?"

"Yes, Adam, good choice!"

And then a spotted animal with a comically long neck.

"Giraffe!"

Something behind him barks.

"Quiet, cat! I mean … dog."

And on and on. As the sun begins to set for the third time ever, God and Adam sit back and enjoy perfect fellowship, and the divine dance begins. Although God infinitely *transcends* Adam, He *intimately* enjoys His new friend fashioned from the dirt.

CROWNED WITH GLORY AND HONOR

God creates (Gen. 1) and God relates (Gen. 2). Both are essential to God's character. We can't sacrifice either of these truths for the sake of the other. If we see God only as *transcendent*, God will seem cold and distant. And if we see God only as *intimate*, then we belittle

Him—making Him our friend but not our Lord. The opening chapters of Genesis describe God as both transcendent and intimate. He's our King and our Friend. Though He could annihilate us with His voice (Gen. 1), He gently breathes life into our nostrils (Gen. 2).

Some people think of God as an angry dad watching our every move with tight lips and arms folded—eager to spank us when we mess up. But the portrait of God in Genesis 1–2 is different. Yes, God has power beyond imagination, and He rules as King over all. "Our God is in the heavens; he does all that he pleases" (Ps. 115:3). But the God of Genesis 1 is the same God eagerly rooting for us in Genesis 2 as He delegates the joyful mission of coruling with Him over His creation.

Psalm 8, which I quoted earlier, says, "When I look at your heavens, the work of your fingers, the moon and the stars, which you have set in place, what is man that you are mindful of him?" (vv. 3–4). But then it goes on to say, "You have made him a little lower than the heavenly beings and *crowned him with glory and honor*" (v. 5).

You wear a crown of glory and honor.

The transcendent King of creation placed it upon your head.

When you look into the mirror and see scars and zits and fat and abuse and loneliness and pain, *Yahweh* sees glory and honor.

SEX BEFORE SEVEN

"Bad little girls get thrown away," Cynthia reasoned when at five years old she found out she was adopted. She didn't understand how her parents could give up their child if they loved her, so Cynthia logically concluded that she was unloved and unworthy—valueless.

All humans crave value; it's in our DNA. So Cynthia tried to satisfy her craving in unhealthy ways. *Maybe sex will give me value,* she thought. *I want to feel happy; I want to feel loved.* A friend of hers had a father with a stash of porn magazines, so the two girls raided the stash and began acting out the sexual activities plastered across the pages. Maybe homosexual sex is where value could be found. The two girls were about seven years old.

When Cynthia was around fourteen, she was sexually abused by a guy in his midtwenties. She then explored value through alcohol, drugs, more sex, and slashing her body with a razor. "I hated myself with a passion," Cynthia recalls. "I didn't need people to put me down. Because I did it fine from the time I woke up until the time I went to bed. The inner dialogue that went on in my head was I was stupid, I was not wanted, I was ugly. The only thing I was good for was sex."

More drugs, more sex, more cutting. When Cynthia was seventeen, she married a boy with a similar past and quickly got pregnant.[3]

Cynthia's story is frighteningly typical. One in every five girls and one in every twenty boys are victimized by sexual abuse. Twenty-eight percent of fourteen- to seventeen-year-olds have been sexually abused on some level as children or teens.[4]

Eating disorders are rapidly increasing among teens and even among young children. Kids under twelve experienced a 119 percent increase in eating disorders between 1999 and 2006, and the statistics continue to rise.[5]

But it doesn't matter where you fall in the statistics. God doesn't see you as garbage, unwanted, fat, or ugly. Where you see defects, God sees a crown and a robe of glory. You are covered in God's fingerprints, with God's breath in your nostrils.

A few years later, Cynthia found Jesus, the One who crowned her with glory and honor. The pain of her past will never fully leave her, but neither will it condemn her. "I have intrinsic value no matter what," Cynthia says, "just because God made me." Though she was unwanted and abused, God has crowned her with beauty and love.

Some of the greatest lies you'll ever believe are told by your eyes as you gaze into a mirror. Lies fueled by your own doubt and a culture that worships a false standard of beauty and worth. Beauty is formed in the eye of the beholder. But your Beholder is God. He made you in His own image; He gave you that crown.

FREEDOM TO LOVE

God is free to do what God wants. He's not subject to anything or anyone higher than Himself. Nobody tells Him that He must do this or must do that.

So when He steps down to rescue and save, to forgive and relate, He does so because He *wants to*.

And God *wants to* because, although He's transcendent, He's also intimate. God desires to be in relationship with His creation, with His creatures—with you. Nobody is twisting His arm. He doesn't relate to us begrudgingly. God stood toe-to-toe with Adam and breathed love into his face because there was nothing God desired more at that moment than to enjoy a vibrant relationship with Adam and, therefore, with you.

Now let me be honest. The God of Genesis 1 I get. It's the God of Genesis 2 that I struggle with. Coming to grips with the God of Genesis 1 is much easier. If God is God, then He must be transcendent.

But what I have a hard time believing is that this same God cares about me. That He delights in me. That He thinks I am more valuable than the hundreds of snowcapped peaks in Colorado. That He can't wait until I wake up so He can see my eyes and hear my voice. That He desires to be in relationship with me—not out of obligation, but out of sheer delight.

I know that He is sovereign. But He wants to be my friend? He wants to have a relationship with me? And He wants this so badly that no matter what I do, He will keep on pursuing me, chasing me, and never give up?

Zephaniah says, "The LORD your God is in your midst, a mighty one who will save; he will rejoice over you with gladness; he will quiet you by his love; he will exult over you with loud singing" (Zeph. 3:17). God sings over us because He crowned us with glory and honor.

Even though we quickly became His enemies.

3

PATRIARCH

SNAKE KILLER

God enjoys our presence. He loves to hear us laugh and sing, and He sings over us with His own songs of joy as we live and eat and work and play. God is not some impatient father fuming with annoyance at His naughty kids. Genesis 2 celebrates an overjoyed Father who adores His masterpieces and smiles when they play in His garden.

But in Genesis 3, God's relationship with creation is forever destroyed. Or at least it should be.

God commands Adam and Eve to enjoy creation—to tend to it, keep it, and reap its bounty. He wants them to find pleasure in His playground and carry on the divine mission: rule over it, develop it, and have sex under palm trees in the sun. God gives them a billion things they can do and one thing they can't do. Don't eat from the Tree of the Knowledge of Good and Evil. Unfortunately, sin is so enticing that the first chance they get, Adam and Eve violate this one rule.[1] The image-bearing pinnacle of creation rebels against its Creator, and the entire cosmos screams in agony.[2]

At this point, God could squash humans with an iron fist, or fry them with a lightning bolt, or take away their image-bearing status and make them slaves of creation instead of rulers over it. This is how some ancient myths depict humanity. The gods create humanity as an afterthought to perform slave labor, providing the gods with their food since they are too lazy to get their own.[3] But *Yahweh* is not like these mythical gods. He is Creator. He is transcendent. He is intimate. He's the God of Genesis 1 *and* Genesis 2.

He's the God of *charis*.

Instead of squashing Adam and Eve or zapping them with lightning, *Yahweh* forgives them. He then sets up a plan to weed out the cancerous evil that has invaded His creation. God will stop at nothing to fix their mess and relate with them.

So in Genesis 3:15, God promises to redeem the world and bring us back to Eden—that place where Creator and creature live in perfect harmony. It goes like this:

> I will put enmity between you and the woman,
>   and between your offspring and her offspring;
> he shall bruise your head,
>   and you shall bruise his heel.

The "you" is Satan and the "woman" is Eve. The offspring of Eve is a particular genealogical line through which God will send the Messiah. Seth, Noah, Shem, and Abraham are all part of that genealogical line of promise, the means through which God will restore creation.

The offspring of Satan are all who oppose God's plan of redemption—Cain, Ham, the Canaanites, and the pharaoh in Egypt who will end up enslaving God's people for over four hundred years. God orchestrates a plan to fix creation by working through the womb of women. Ultimately, a descendant of Eve will "bruise" (or "crush") the head of Satan. That's the promise of Genesis 3:15. And that's why this verse is the first of many so-called messianic promises of the Bible.

Spoiler alert: Jesus is that offspring of Eve, the snake crusher who will redeem creation and conquer evil.

Of all the ways that God could have saved us, He chose to work through the womb of women to raise up an image bearer who would crush the head of Satan so that God could regain that Eden-like relationship with His masterpieces. Keep that in mind when you read the Bible. *Everything* hinges upon that promise.

But before grace raises up Jesus through Mary's womb, it seeks out an idolater from the pagan town of Ur—a burgeoning city in Mesopotamia, a land radiating with wickedness and depravity. And God's Genesis 3:15 promise lurches into action.

ABRAHAM: FAITHFUL SAINT OR TROPHY OF GRACE?

Abraham is one of the most well-known figures in the Bible. He's also among the most misunderstood. When I was growing up in the church, the name *Abraham* conjured up images of obedience, faithfulness, and unswerving morality. Here's a guy who had it all together. He walked with God. Prayed to God. Fled from sin. And when God demanded that he kill his own son, Abraham eagerly went to the mountain with knife in hand. *It's no wonder,* I thought, *that God was able to use him.* Abraham was perfect—or pretty close to it.

But after studying and teaching the Old Testament several times, I realized that very little of my childhood view of Abraham was true. Yes, he was sort of faithful and did obey from time to time, and yes, it is true that Abraham went to sacrifice Isaac at God's command. But none of this can be rightly understood apart from grace—God's stubborn delight in stubborn people.

Far from being a faithful saint, Abraham is a trophy of God's scandalous delight.

When God first meets Abraham, he is a pagan idolater. Abraham is bowing down to idols, offering sacrifices to different gods, and having sex with temple prostitutes so that a moon god named Nanna will show him favor.[4]

Some religious traditions are offended at this picture of Abraham. They say that Abraham left his pagan ways *before* God called him to pack his bags for Palestine—God helps those who help themselves. But according to the Bible, God calls Abraham *while* he is engulfed in idolatry.[5] Perhaps he is on his knees before a pagan statue or with a temple prostitute when God says, "That's the guy I want to use to save the world." You can't domesticate *charis*. It runs wild and free.

Then, before Abraham has the chance to do anything good, God promises to give him the land of Canaan, make him a mighty nation, and bless people of other nations through him (Gen. 12:1–3). This promise is an *unconditional* promise; there's nothing Abraham does to earn it, no conditions he needs to fulfill in order to ensure its fulfillment. And this promise forms the backbone for the entire Bible.

God forms the nation of Israel, delivers it from the Red Sea, conquers the land of Canaan, raises up King David, speaks through the prophets, sends His Son, Jesus Christ, and saves you and me, all because of His daring promise to a wicked man from Ur.

Our salvation rests upon God's unyielding commitment to a pagan idolater.

After God calls him, Abraham does do some good things. He believes God's word in Genesis 15. He has faith that God will give him a son in Genesis 17. And he offers up Isaac in response to God's command in Genesis 22.

But Abraham's life is also littered with doubt, fear, unfaithfulness, and lying. For instance, immediately after God promises to give him the land of Canaan and make him a mighty nation (Gen. 12:1–3), Abraham flees to the land of Egypt and nearly loses his wife by lying to another man, telling him she is his sister (Gen. 12:10–20). If God's promises rested upon Abraham's behavior, then we would all be in hell.

In Genesis 16, Abraham believes that God will give him a son, but he doesn't think it can come through his wife, Sarah. *She's too old. I'm too old,* Abraham thinks. *It would be a miracle for her to conceive a child. God will have to provide a son through another woman.* So Abraham does what any childless old man would have done in that day. He takes his concubine Hagar, has sex with her, and tries to manufacture God's promise through his own effort. Abraham's world-class faith that's put on a pedestal in Sunday school is apparently mingled with quite a bit of doubt.

Then, while hanging out in the desert, Abraham experiences a bit of déjà vu. He's afraid that the men of the city will see his beautiful wife, kill him, and take her away. So he lies *again*, telling them she's his sister and not his wife (Gen. 20). Again, Abraham nearly squanders the promise that God would make him into a mighty nation *through Sarah*.

Do you ever get discouraged about your ongoing struggle with gossip, pride, porn, or alcohol? I imagine Abraham did too. Apparently, he had an ongoing struggle with lying.

It's no wonder that the apostle Paul, when reaching for an Old Testament example of grace, went straight for Abraham. After writing three chapters about God's unconditional love through Jesus (Rom. 1:18–3:30), Paul summed up his argument in one short phrase: "[God] justifies the ungodly" (Rom. 4:5). How do we know this? Just look at Abraham:

> For what does the Scripture say? "Abraham believed God, and it was counted to him as righteousness." Now to the one who works, his wages are not counted as a gift [*charis*] but as his due. And to the one who does not work but believes in him who justifies the ungodly, his faith is counted as righteousness. (Rom. 4:3–5)

Abraham does nothing to earn God's *charis*. God doesn't love Abraham because of what Abraham does or doesn't do. God loves Abraham because of God.

GOD WALKS ALONE

God's most subversive act of grace, however, intrudes into Abraham's life in Genesis 15. Remember, in Genesis 12 God promises to give

Abraham the land of Canaan, make him a mighty nation, and bless the nations through him. Now in Genesis 15 God publicly confirms His promises through a covenant ceremony. If Genesis 12 is the engagement, then Genesis 15 is the wedding day.

The covenant ceremony that God and Abraham perform involves an ancient ritual that seems strange to us, but it was common in Abraham's day. Genesis describes it like this:

> And he said to him, "I am the LORD who brought you out from Ur of the Chaldeans to give you this land to possess." But he said, "O Lord GOD, how am I to know that I shall possess it?" He said to him, "Bring me a heifer three years old, a female goat three years old, a ram three years old, a turtledove, and a young pigeon." And he brought him all these, cut them in half, and laid each half over against the other. (Gen. 15:7–10)

Bizarre, I know. But back in Abraham's time, this was a typical ritual that two people would carry out in order to confirm an agreement.[6] Let's say, for instance, a guy named Winston wanted to buy a camel from a guy named Wayne. In exchange for the camel, Winston agreed to let Wayne marry his daughter. Winston could walk away with the camel right then, but his daughter was only eleven years old. She couldn't be married for another two years. (Yes, thirteen was marital age back then.) Wayne was a bit worried that Winston might go back on his promise, and so in order to confirm the promise, Wayne and Winston each took an animal, killed it, and cut its body in two. Then they divided the two animals, and both Wayne and Winston walked between the bloody halves of the carcasses.

Wayne assured Winston that he would give up his camel. Winston assured Wayne that he would give up his daughter. And they walked between the bloody halves of the animals to proclaim, "May I be like this dead animal if I go back on my word." That was the purpose of the dead animals: to remind the two people that they'd be slaughtered if they broke their promise.

Back to Genesis 15. God has already promised to bless Abraham and all families of the earth, which includes you if you're a non-Jewish believer in Jesus (Gen. 12:1–3). So Abraham kills five animals and divides their dead bodies so that he and God can walk between the parts. In doing so, God will keep His word to bless Abraham, and Abraham will keep his word to be faithful and not sin. If either one fails to keep his side of the agreement, may he be cursed—slaughtered—like these five dead animals.

But God walks alone.

When it comes time to walk between the bloody parts, God causes Abraham to fall into a deep sleep, while God alone passes between the carcasses:

> As the sun was going down, a deep sleep fell on Abram. And behold, dreadful and great darkness fell upon him.... When the sun had gone down and it was dark, behold, a smoking fire pot and a flaming torch passed between these pieces. (Gen. 15:12, 17)

PORN STARS, PROSTITUTES, AND THE SCANDALOUS GRACE OF GOD

Judah was a patriarch, the head of one of the twelve tribes of Israel. And Judah was one of the shadiest characters in the Bible. If Judah moved into the house next door, you'd pack your bags and sell your house. You wouldn't risk the danger. You've got a wife and kids to protect.

We don't know a whole lot about Judah, but there is one chapter where Judah takes center stage: Genesis 38—one of the filthiest sections in the Bible. It's one of those chapters you never really hear about in church. Whenever I teach it to my college students, I feel like I need their parents to sign a waiver beforehand.

But God gave us the Bible with all its grit and gunk, so here's the uncut version of Genesis 38. It's one of the most unsettling stories of grace in the Bible.

The story begins with Judah lusting over a Canaanite woman. He then has sex with her, and in time she ends up giving him three sons. Judah's firstborn half-Canaanite son named Er marries a Canaanite girl named Tamar, but Er does something stupid (we don't know what), and God kills him (v. 7). Then Er's brother Onan has sex with Tamar to raise up a son for his dead brother but ends up spilling his "semen on the ground" (v. 9), which is evil in the sight of the Lord.[7] So God kills him, too.

Lust, illicit sex, two dead sons, and an ancient lesson in birth control. If my Sunday school teacher told us this story growing up, I might have actually read the Bible in junior high.

Judah is left with his widowed Canaanite daughter-in-law, Tamar, and he tells her to wait until his youngest son grows up so that she can marry him. *Yeah right! God keeps killing off your loser sons. I'm not waiting around to become a three-time widow,* Tamar probably thinks. So Tamar and Judah part ways.

A few years later, Judah is strolling by a village and sees a sexy prostitute sitting near the city gate. Judah, being the charmer that he is, breaks out his best ancient pickup line: "Here now, let me come in to you" (38:16 NASB). And yes, "come in to you" means just what you think. Judah has sex with the prostitute, but since he has left his wallet at home, he pays her on credit (Gen. 38:17–18).

Stay with me. This story is all about grace, I promise you.

Come to find out, it isn't a prostitute Judah slept with. It's his daughter-in-law, Tamar! She dressed up as a prostitute *so that* her father-in-law would sleep with her. But it gets worse. Judah should have taken birth control lessons from Onan because he not only had sex with his daughter-in-law but impregnated her as well. As the story concludes, Tamar and Judah end up having twins—Perez and Zerah. And you thought you had a bad week!

But God takes this crass story and turns it into a *charis* story.

Notice where Genesis 38 occurs. It's placed right after Genesis 37 and just before Genesis 39. Brilliant observation, I know. But the placement of Genesis 38 is significant because Genesis 37 begins the "Joseph story," which runs all the way to the end of Genesis. Joseph is known for his unswerving obedience. He is one of the most moral characters in the entire Bible.

But Joseph isn't mentioned in Genesis 38. Although Joseph is the star in Genesis 37, he's completely left out of Genesis 38, and then he pops up again as the main character in Genesis 39–50. The story of Judah and Tamar, therefore, *interrupts* the Joseph story. And Judah and Tamar's intrusion into Joseph's story is intentional. Here's why.

Moses deliberately inserted Judah's debacle into Joseph's story in order to contrast the two characters. The difference could not be greater. Joseph flees sexual lust, while Judah sprints toward it. Joseph is morally impeccable, while Judah is a moral train wreck.

So why the contrast?

GENEALOGY OF GRACE

If you read the Bible *morally*, then you might conclude that the contrast shows us how to live moral lives like Joseph and how not to live immoral lives like Judah. While there may be some truth to this—we should all seek to be like Joseph and definitely should not be like Judah—that's not the main point of the contrast.

The contrast is messianic. It shows us that God's rock-solid promise to redeem His wayward children and to be in relationship with His people—to love us, forgive us, enjoy us—cannot be thwarted by wickedness. God will relate with us. God will bring His people back to Eden.

God will do this by His grace. God's promised Messiah—the One who will kill the snake and redeem the world (Gen. 3:15)—will come through Judah, even though everything in our transactional bones wants to see God use Joseph, the morally superior choice.

God deliberately selects the genealogical line of Judah, not Joseph, to bring forth the Savior—the snake-crushing seed of Eve. According to Jesus's genealogy,

> Abraham was the father of Isaac, and Isaac the
> father of Jacob, and Jacob the father of Judah and
> his brothers, and Judah the father of Perez and
> Zerah *by Tamar, and Perez the father of* Hezron.
> (Matt. 1:2–3)

God hand selects Perez—the illegitimate son from an illicit affair between a father-in-law and daughter-in-law dressed up as harlot—to be a part of His plan to redeem the world.

God deliberately gets His hands dirty by molding Judah's mess into a conduit of grace, because God is in the business of working through our messes. Grace does not mean that God encourages sin or discourages righteousness. Not at all (Rom. 6:1–2). Nor does it mean that God saves people apart from faith in Christ. But it does mean that no mess, no failure, no broken marriage, no affair, no night with a prostitute can prevent God from using you—an image-bearing masterpiece, frail and flawed, forever loved.

Grace pursues; grace transforms; grace molds porn stars into objects of delight. Grace means that God seeks out repugnant sinners—the Judahs of the world—and uses them to redeem wicked people.

And we are Judah.

4

TENT

LOW AND DESPISED

God is in the business of using unusable people, and Judah is only one of many examples. The entire Bible is filled with social outcasts, slaves, prostitutes, and thugs—all of whose lives are delightfully wrecked by a gracious Creator who enjoys wrecking undelightful people. God isn't just able to use messed-up sinners to accomplish His plan. He actually prefers to. "God chose what is low and despised in the world … so that no human being might boast in the presence of God" (1 Cor. 1:28–29).

This is why the book of Exodus is filled with sinners and outcasts who become conduits of grace when God liberates His people from Egypt. If you haven't noticed this, you may have been reading the Old Testament through a thick moral lens—looking for heroes and saints to emulate, instead of a gracious God to thank.

Or it's because you're a man.

I'm embarrassed to admit that it was not until three years after I completed a PhD in Bible that I noticed God using a bunch of *women* to rescue His people from slavery in Egypt. God's choice of female redeemers is a backhanded slap to the patriarchal, male-centered culture He was working within.

ESTROGEN

In the ancient world, women were considered inferior to men and were subject to much oppression. A woman was property: the daughter of her father or the wife of her husband. "I am a daughter, I am a bride, I am a spouse, I am a housekeeper," was the mantra sung by women as they slogged through life with little apparent worth.[1] Women existed in order to bear children, keep a good home, and in some cases brew beer for the local tavern, where the men would guzzle ale, listen to music, and enjoy the company of prostitutes. Oh yes, I almost forgot. Women made good prostitutes as well.

But God created people in His image, "male *and* female" (Gen. 1:27). Women reflect God's image just as much as men. Or, should I say, men as much as women. You cannot see God's image wholly in a monastery.

In Exodus 1 we find the Israelites living a good life in Egypt thanks to Joseph's rise to power in the foreign land.[2] But shortly after, we learn that a new pharaoh came to power who "did not know Joseph" and therefore enslaved the Israelites.[3] *Yahweh*'s promise is suspended in midair as Abraham's offspring are enslaved in a foreign land.

Step by step, God continues to work out his Genesis 3:15 promise, and heaven rumbles with a furious joy.

God's grace first descends upon a bunch of unnamed midwives in Exodus 1. In order to halt the rapid birthrate of the Israelites, Pharaoh orders the Israelite midwives to kill off all the firstborn male children. But the "midwives feared God" (Exod. 1:21) and oppose the command of the king.

In the midst of the attempted slaughter, one particular woman hides her boy to keep him from being killed (Exod. 2:1–2). After three months she can no longer keep him a secret, so she slips him into a basket and sends him floating down the Nile River. The boy's sister, Miriam, watches him until he bumps into Pharaoh's daughter, who is bathing in the river. Miriam suggests to Pharaoh's daughter that one of the Israelite women could nurse the child, and she agrees. So Miriam finds the baby's own mother to nurse her son, Moses—a refreshing ironic twist in the midst of infanticidal horrors.

After Moses grows up, he kills a man and buries his body in the sand. Out of fear, he flees from Egypt to a land called Midian, where he encounters seven daughters of a pagan priest named Reuel, who provides Moses with shelter and food. Moses ends up marrying Zipporah, one of Reuel's daughters, and they have a child named Gershom. His parents are a murderous ex-slave turned refugee and the daughter of a pagan priest.

We don't know much about Moses's wife, Zipporah. What we do know is that she saved Moses's life (Exod. 4:24–26). Even though God demanded that all male children were to be circumcised, apparently Moses forgot to operate on Gershom. One day, Moses is strolling along with his family when all of a sudden God is seconds away from destroying him for not circumcising his son. So Zipporah intervenes and saves Moses's life. That is, she cuts off Gershom's foreskin with a flint rock and tosses the piece of skin at Moses's feet. (I know, I wish I could have seen the look on Gershom's face too: "Mom, what do you plan on doing with that sharp rock?")

The story raises more questions than it answers, but one thing is clear: God's grace invaded the desert with unwelcomed splendor and targeted a bunch of undervalued and oppressed women. Were it not for Zipporah, Moses would have never lived to see the Red Sea divide in two.

Midwives, female slaves, the daughter of a wicked king, and an African woman wielding a very sharp rock. The only ounce of testosterone God uses here is stored up in the glands of an abandoned child named Moses.

But God does end up using a few men in Exodus. Along with Moses, who grows into a tongue-tied murderer, God also uses Aaron, Moses's brother, who will lead the nation into idolatry that results in the deaths of three thousand people. God doesn't help those who help themselves. God creates righteousness like the stars—out of thin air.

DELIVERANCE

The entire book of Exodus is shaped by grace. Grace is seen in the people God uses, the people God redeems, and the way God redeems them. If there ever was clear evidence that God saves people based on who *He* is and not on what *we* have done, it's the exodus from Egypt. God doesn't rescue His people from Egypt because they are righteous. They aren't fasting, praying, or even living righteously while in slavery. They aren't on their knees, seeking the Lord. In fact, the Bible tells us they are on their knees, worshipping idols.[4]

The Israelite slaves are freed from the clutches of oppression because God is moved with pity for His people. "I have surely seen the

affliction of my people who are in Egypt and have heard their cry.…
I know their sufferings.… The cry of the people of Israel has come
to me, and I have also seen the oppression with which the Egyptians
oppress them" (Exod. 3:7, 9; see also 4:31; 6:5). God's power is released
on account of His compassion, not Israel's righteousness.

God is transcendent. He has the raw ability to part seas in two.
God is also intimate. He'll bring you through the stormy seas and
embrace you on the other side. He doesn't help you *if* you first muster
the will to help yourself. God rescues sinners, losers, victims—those
who *know* they can't help themselves. And this is why God delivers
Israel from Egypt. Israel is unlovable. So God loves the Israelites.

Grace is what moves God to use a bunch of women to raise up
a redeemer. Grace is what compels God to rescue His people from
slavery. And grace is what kindles God's passion to drum up a plan
for Israel to build a tent.

HOLY TENT

A tent?

Yes, you read that correctly. One of the most unread and under-
appreciated sections of the Bible comes at the end of Exodus—chapters
25–31 and 35–40, to be exact. Although these latter chapters lack the
thrill of parting seas and flaming mountaintops, there's a glowing pearl
of grace hidden at the end of Exodus. And it's buried in a tent.

What's so exciting about a tent? *I don't even like to camp,* you
may think.

It's more than a tent, actually. You may know it better as the
tabernacle. And here's why this tent was vital for Israel's existence.

God is holy, and we are not, so putting the two together makes a dangerous equation. Holiness means that God is pure, that He is different, that He is—to use the standard definition—set apart. And when a holy God encounters unholy people, the holiness of God annihilates the unholy people. "Go down and warn the people," God tells Moses from the top of Sinai, "lest they break through to the LORD to look and *many of them perish*" (Exod. 19:21). If unholy people look upon a holy God, they vanish like tax dollars in California.

And they know this. "Do not let God speak to us, lest we die" (Exod. 20:19), the people cry out. Centuries later, the prophet Isaiah finds himself in the same fatal (and probably fetal) position. "Woe is me! For I am [ruined]; for I am a man of unclean lips, and I dwell in the midst of a people of unclean lips; for my eyes have seen the King, the LORD of hosts!" (Isa. 6:5).[5] God Himself says, "Man shall not see me and live" (Exod. 33:20).

When people encounter God and are *not* annihilated, these are exceptions to the rule—radical acts of grace, if you will. Typically, when unholy people come face-to-face with a holy God, His holiness is too much to bear. They are obliterated.

This is where the tent comes in. God cannot dwell with sinful people, but God desires to dwell with sinful people. So He comes up with a plan to have them build a tent, or *tabernacle*, so that He can dwell with His people without annihilating them. This is why there are walls and rooms in the tent. Thick curtains separate the inner room, where God dwells, from the outer room, where the priests hang out. The outer room is again separated from the outer courts, where the common people can visit. All in all, these degrees of separation are designed to wall off God's holy presence from the unholy Israelites. You can think of it as a gracious safety measure.

That's what Exodus 25–31 is all about. The details aren't that exciting. But the theological point is astonishing. The instructions to build a tabernacle show that our holy God desires to be in relationship with us—even if it means living in a tent. We don't go to God; God comes to us. We can try to build a tower into the heavens to reach Him … um, or maybe not. We have a God who is far, yet very near. Transcendent and intimate. He ventures into our murky space to relate with us. After all, you've got to plunge your hands into the sewage to fix the drain.

WEDDING NIGHT AFFAIR

The God who dwells in heaven chooses to dwell in a tent to be closer to us. But the story gets more scandalous.

The book of Exodus doesn't end in Exodus 31. It ends in Exodus 40. And what happens between Exodus 31 and 40 is outrageous. After God gives a seven-chapter blueprint of how to build a tabernacle (Exod. 25–31), Moses tells a brief story about what happened to the Israelites while he was up with God on Mount Sinai. The incident occurs in Exodus 32–34. We know it as the story of the golden calf.

When Moses climbs the mountain, he leaves Aaron in charge. But the people grow impatient and want to replace Moses and God with a statue of a golden calf that will lead them to the Promised Land. "Up, make us gods who shall go before us," they command Aaron. "As for this Moses, the man who brought us up out of the land of Egypt, we do not know what has become of him" (Exod.

32:1). Aaron complies, and according to his version of the story, he takes the people's gold jewelry, tosses it into a fire, and lo and behold, "out came this calf" (Exod. 32:24).

"Really, Aaron? You just tossed it in?"

"Seriously, it just popped right out! You've got to believe me. I had nothing to do with it."

So, within a few days of their zealous commitment to obey everything God commands (Exod. 19:3–8), the Israelites, led by their high priest, offer up sacrifices and perform sexual orgies to honor a god made by their own hands.[6] If God's covenant with His people is like a marriage, then the Israelites are committing adultery on their wedding night.

What will God do now with His plan to build a tent? What would you do if your spouse got up in the middle of the night during your honeymoon and had sex with the person next door?

Me too. Good thing God is not like us. God's commitment to us is fundamentally different from and more stubbornly unconditional than our commitment to our spouses or our commitment to God. God has an Edenic desire to be in relationship with humans—at all cost. So against all intuition, contradicting all forms of merit and transaction, undercutting our natural sense of justice and fairness, knocking over our towers of Babel, and obliterating the social norms of royalty, power, and the way gods are supposed to act—*Yahweh* builds a tent.

Notice the structure:

> *Yahweh* desires to dwell in a tent among His people (Exod. 25–31).

His people commit spiritual adultery (Exod. 32–34).

Yahweh dwells in a tent among His people (Exod. 35–40).

Put differently:

Yahweh desires to relate with you.

You have sex with your neighbor's spouse.

Yahweh reaches down and relates with you.

God desires to dwell with sinful people, and we must let this seep into our bones. God could stand at the gates of heaven and forgive the Israelites. He could clap His hands, mutter a chant, or fold His arms and nod His head, and *if He willed it*, the Israelites would be forgiven. God could show them leniency or simply accept them unconditionally, and He would give them a *type* of grace, but it would not be the stuff of the Bible. It would not be *charis*.

The *charis* of God furiously pursues wicked people. *Charis* stubbornly delights in repugnant rebels. And God's *charis* moves Him to descend with joy into the tent so that He can be in an intimate relationship with His image-bearing—albeit calf-worshipping—masterpieces of creation: "Then the cloud covered the tent of meeting, and the glory of the LORD filled the tabernacle" (Exod. 40:34).

God's presence—the "cloud of glory"—now resides with His people, and the smell of Eden wafts through the desert.

JOURNEY BACK TO EDEN

What I love about the garden of Eden is that it's not just a thing of the past. Sin tried to trip up God's race toward sinners, but He hurdled right over it by passing between dead animals. Eden is what He created us for, and God isn't interested in a plan B. The tent is just one more reminder that God will get what He wants. He will bring us back to the garden.

The details of the tabernacle decor are often passed over, but they help us plumb the depths of God's grace. Let's take a quick tour.

Images of spiritual creatures called cherubim are embroidered into the curtains that hang throughout the tabernacle, and two golden cherubim sit on top of the ark of the covenant inside the Holy of Holies. In the middle of the sanctuary stands a six-branched lampstand with images of flowers, calyxes, and almond blossoms at the ends of the branches—a regular "tree of light." Across from the lampstand is the bread of the Presence. The entire tabernacle is covered with an abundance of gold, as well as silver, bronze, and a precious gemstone known as onyx.

Glowing beauty, copious vegetation, and luxurious gemstones fit for royalty.

The Israelites will later replace the portable tabernacle with a stationary temple under King Solomon, who increases the vegetation imagery by carving "engraved figures of cherubim and palm trees and open flowers, in the inner and outer rooms" (1 Kings 6:29). Solomon also builds two massive statues of cherubim (seventeen feet tall) to stand on each side of the ark of the covenant inside the Holy of Holies, where God dwells. And pomegranates dangle from the garments of the priests, who *work* and *keep* the tabernacle.

Work and keep? Sounds like an odd choice of verbs to describe the priestly duties in the tabernacle, but these are the words used throughout the Bible (such as Num. 3:7–8) and—follow me here—these are the same words used in tandem to describe what Adam and Eve were commanded to do in Eden. "The LORD God took the man and put him in the garden of Eden to *work* [*abad*] it and *keep* [*shamar*] it" (Gen. 2:15). The only times "work and keep" are used together in the Bible are in Eden (Gen. 2:15) and the tabernacle (for example, Num. 3:7–8).[7] When you think of the tabernacle, you should think of Eden.

Cherubim guarding the presence of God (as in Gen. 2) in a sanctuary decked out with vegetation imagery, where priests work and keep the sacred space where God resides—need I say more? The tabernacle is designed to represent the garden of Eden, the place where Creator and creation enjoyed harmonious fellowship, perfect relationship, utopian *shalom*.

Ever since Adam and Eve were expelled from Eden (where God dwelled), God has been on a mission to reclaim this Eden-like relationship with His people, and the building of the tabernacle is one major step toward this goal. Calf-worshipping fornicators notwithstanding.

GOD IS ALWAYS DOING HIS DEVOTIONS

Too often, we think of our relationship with God in terms of how we are pursuing Him. If someone were to ask you, "How are you doing spiritually?" you would probably answer in light of how many hours you have spent praying or reading your Bible (or not), how many times you've witnessed to your coworkers, or how many days it's been since you've looked at porn. All of these are important, yet they all focus on *you* and *your* pursuit of God.

Grace, on the other hand, means that God is pursuing you. That God forgives you. That God sanctifies you.

When you are apathetic toward God, He is never apathetic toward you.

When you don't desire to pray and talk to God, He never grows tired of talking to you.

When you forget to read your Bible and listen to God, He is always listening to you.

Grace means that your spirituality is upheld by God's stubborn enjoyment of you. So we should learn to speak of our spirituality in the passive voice—not as someone who acts but primarily as someone who has been acted upon by a God who defines Himself as the One who "justifies the ungodly" (Rom. 4:5).

Grace is what compels God to find a stubborn delight in dwelling with calf-worshipping sinners who committed adultery on their wedding night.

5

KING

HOLY HOODLUMS

In the fall of 2011, I had a surreal experience. I attended a Christian conference at an upscale hotel, where theologians read papers to one another. Yes, these scholars are brilliant. But literally, they read papers to each other. I attend this conference every year. It's a lot like going to the zoo. Many animals are brilliant, though they live boring lives—detached from the real world. I especially like the monkeys. They're the most brilliant, but watch out for the poo. The similarities are endless.

The conference is held just before Thanksgiving, this year in downtown San Francisco—one of the most depraved cities in the country. It happened that my friend and well-known speaker Francis Chan was working in the inner city one mile from where the conference was held. So after listening to theological papers for two days, I spent two hours with Francis in the inner city. I visited City Impact, the ministry where Francis was serving at the time. After slurping down some tasty Vietnamese pho, we delivered food and toiletries to impoverished people living in low-income housing in the inner city—three blocks from the upscale hotel where our Christians were reading papers to one another.

The contrast between the two days at the conference and two hours in the inner city was mystifying.

That afternoon, I met lots of cool people in the Boyd, the name given to the low-income apartment complex where Francis and I distributed goods. The tenants lived in one-room flats with a bathroom down the hall, and they all lacked basic necessities in life. Food, clothing, love, toiletries, and much more.

One woman, Lisa, lacked more than food. She lacked four fingers on her right hand and got by with just a thumb. She also lacked her two kids, who were taken away from her and now live in Texas.

Moses, the man down the hall, hadn't seen his family members in almost three years, but glowing with jubilance, he told us that he was going to see them in a week at an upcoming Thanksgiving meal. For Moses, that Thanksgiving would be more than suburban gluttony. He was truly thankful that he'd see his family, and his thankfulness welled up in his eyes as he imaged the reunion.

Everyone I met lacked hope. Pounded by the storms of life, the tenants of the Boyd lost all hope many years ago. But Francis and I were able to kindle a quiet ember deep within them by inviting them to a Thanksgiving banquet, where they would be fed steak, shrimp, and pasta (Lisa's request). More than that, they would be waited upon by the volunteers—including Francis. A Christian celebrity waiting hand and foot on a bunch of marginalized ruffians who don't know who he is. Brilliant! I wanted to take them to see the monkeys, but we didn't have time.

I was most affected that afternoon by a woman named Shelia Wheeler. Shelia also lived in the Boyd, but she got a $175/month stipend to act as a liaison between the city and the tenants whenever needs arose. If the carpet needed cleaning, she'd get it cleaned. If the washer needed fixing, she'd find someone to fix it. (She didn't have to worry about this, though, because there were no washers or dryers in the building.) Shelia was their advocate, their friend, and their source of hope. In many ways she was their "pastor," and she laughed out loud when I told her that. Yeah, she didn't make enough money to be a pastor anyway.

I was quickly impressed by Shelia's love for the outcasts living in the Boyd. But what she said about her stipend sent shivers down my spine and into my wallet. Although Shelia was living in grinding poverty, she told us that she tried to funnel her $175 stipend back into the apartment building to improve the living conditions for other tenants. She wanted to give it away. Unconditionally. But the city wouldn't let her. She must—against her will—keep her robust salary and spend it on herself.

Those two days at the conference and the two hours in the inner city bled with irony. I listened to dozens of theological papers read by brilliant theologians, but I learned more about God, Christianity, and the church in the two hours I spent with the hoodlums of inner-city San Francisco. Proverbs says that "whoever mocks the poor insults his Maker" (17:5), and Jesus said, "As you did it to one of the least of these my brothers"—caring for the poor—"you did it to me" (Matt. 25:40). However you slice it, the Bible identifies God with the poor and the outcast. As I left the Boyd and its beautiful residents, I wondered, *Who is teaching whom?*

The Old Testament smells a lot like the inner city of San Francisco. God conquers Satan through the wombs of prostitutes, outcasts, and a Moabite widow—folks who would be right at home in a low-income apartment of a depraved city.

FROM EGYPT TO CANAAN

Israel's journey from Egypt to Canaan is peppered with strange events: the earth swallows a clan, almond blossoms sprout from a rod, and a donkey opens its mouth to argue with a wayward prophet. Who says the Bible is dull? Finally, at the end of forty years, the nation arrives on the edge of the Promised Land, where Moses preaches a series of deathbed sermons, which have been collected in a book we know as Deuteronomy.

After Moses dies, God raises up Joshua to lead Israel into the land of Canaan, where he's commanded to drive out all its inhabitants. But there is grace in the midst of violence, as God visits the pagan town of Jericho and touches the heart of a loose woman making a living as a harlot. As we have seen, women were degraded in the ancient world. Women who were widowed or divorced had an especially tough time surviving. Oftentimes, they sold themselves into slavery or rented out their bodies for sex in order to put food on the table.

Such is the case with Rahab. Destitute, lonely, hopeless. She's outcast, shamed, and lives with the stigma of being nothing more than a shell of momentary pleasure for creepy men.

Perfect candidate for God's grace.

Through Rahab's encounter with two Israelite spies (Josh. 2), God removes her sin as far as the east is from the west and welcomes her into His family. And I don't just mean the family of Israelites.

God actually grafts Rahab into Jesus's family tree.[1] We don't know too many details about Rahab's postconversion life, but we do know that she married an Israelite named Salmon and that they had at least one kid together. His name was Boaz—the great-granddaddy of King David, the man through whom God would send His Son, Jesus Christ.

God continues to conquer Satan through the genealogical line of a sex addict named Judah, a whore named Tamar, a bastard named Perez, and a streetwalker named Rahab. Jesus's family tree would grow quite well in downtown San Francisco.

WARRIOR

The book of Judges traces Israel's moral decline in Canaan, and it's a gnarly book. If I ever see that my students are getting bored with the Bible, I read them a story from Judges and they perk right up. Were it put to film, Judges would be rated R, and I suspect that squeamish viewers would faint somewhere between Ehud thrusting his dagger into Eglon's gut and Jael smashing a spike through Sisera's skull.[2] Quentin Tarantino would find much material for another excessively violent movie (*Inglourious Judges? Reservoir Jews?*). The script is there, divinely written into the story of Judges. Yet the book is all about grace.

Like much of the Old Testament, the book of Judges has become a victim of moralization. Pick up any children's Bible and you're bound to find glowing portraits of Gideon, Barak, Samson, and other heroes to emulate. But skim the stories and you'll see that these warriors don't have a moral compass, or if they do, it's always pointing in the wrong direction. In our attempt to be like the heroes of old, we should consider what that would actually mean. Such imitation could land us on death row.

Barak, for instance, is a coward. He doesn't trust the prophetic word spoken through Deborah, and when it comes time to go to war, two women (Deborah and Jael) shoulder the Israelite victory—a blatant critique of Barak's failure to cowboy up.

The next warrior is Gideon, the bipolar Baal worshipper from the tribe of Manasseh. One day he's fearful and cowardly. The next he's vengeful and proud. He ultimately leads his people into the same idolatry he is commissioned to banish. And when asked if he will become king, his hyperspiritual response ("the LORD will rule over you"[3]) is exposed as fraudulent by the birth of his son. Abimelech, the name Gideon gives his firstborn, means "my father" (namely, Gideon) "is king." So much for false humility.

And then there's Samson. From beginning to end, Samson's life is littered with sin. He has an insatiable appetite for sex and repeatedly satisfies it with Philistine women. He's ignorant of his high calling and violates God's instruction every chance he gets. He's vengeful, obtuse, self-centered, and enslaved to his sexual passions. In his last breath, he has the chance to use his strength for the glory of God but instead calls upon the Creator to help him pay back the Philistines for poking out his two eyes (Judg. 16:28).[4] If selflessness is inherent to heroism, then Samson has just lost his badge of honor. Far from being a character to emulate, Samson is just another Judah.

These warriors are moral train wrecks, but in the public eye, they are larger-than-life. Samson rips apart a lion with his bare hands. Jephthah could be a US Navy SEAL. And Gideon is quite the ladies' man, I'll give him that. But does he have to marry them all?[5] These guys are made for the stage. They have a theatrical presence that bolsters widespread fame. They get the job done and do it with pomp and flare. If they started a church, it would become mega within months.

Most of all, these arrogant warriors are conduits of grace. God uses them all to carry out His will and establish His kingdom on earth. God doesn't employ Gideon because he's righteous, but despite his unrighteousness. The book of Judges is not about God using people who have it all together, or doing powerful things through powerful people. It's about God using cowards to do courageous feats, the violent to accomplish peace, and women to strengthen the spineless backbone of a patriarchal culture. These testosterone-rich warriors have much talent. But please, mind the poo.

GRACIOUS EVIL

Grace sometimes hides its tender favor in order to execute God's plan of redemption. Not all the warriors are redeemed by God's grace, yet grace is what empowers them, despite their sin, to carry out God's will—sometimes unknowingly (Judg. 14:4).

This is why your divorce, your addiction, your enslavement to porn, or years of sticking your finger down your throat to match up to some arbitrary standard of beauty can all be woven into the fabric of God's plan of redemption. God doesn't cause sin. He mourns it. He despises it. But through His gracious power, He's able to use it. No one and no sin can outrun God's grace. *Charis* has no leash.

God redeems the horrors of divorce, for instance, to reinforce goodness in His people. My parents divorced when I was ten years old. It was tragic. But looking back, I can see that the divorce has shaped my desire to be a committed husband and loving father. And now I can truly enter the pain of and comfort those suffering from a divorce.

A friend of mine nearly wrecked his marriage through a hidden addiction to porn. Now, after repentance, he's able to minister to a massive group of men who are in the thick of their addiction and on the brink of wrecking their own marriages.

Another friend has three seminary degrees, a PhD in Bible, a godly wife, and a promising career as a Christian scholar. A few years ago, he was arrested by the Feds for soliciting two teenage girls for sex through an advertisement that popped up while he was watching porn. His wife left him, his boss fired him, and, were it not for grace, God would have fired him too. Looking back, he now sees that his job was his idol and that his workaholic tendencies fostered his sexual addiction. His life is now a sauna of pain, but he's no longer addicted to porn. He no longer idolizes his career. He's in a better place with God *because* God let him experience the destruction of sin. And now, with new life, he can come to the aid of many others sliding down the same slippery slope.

God hijacks and bends evil to work peace and healing. If God were only a God of justice, He could punish evil but do no more. Only a God of grace can use our evil to work His good. God's grace is so much bigger than our sin. Sometimes He'll let us pursue our idolatry until it kills us. Then He will resurrect us and turn our evil into testimonies of God's grace.

IMMIGRANT

Despite their sin, God used the judges to continue His plan of redemption. But the most precious movement of grace was happening off the stage.

The book of Ruth belongs inside the book of Judges. Its story is set during "the days when the judges ruled" (Ruth 1:1), and this is important for understanding its message of grace. The contrast between Ruth and the warriors could not be greater, much like the incongruity I felt in downtown San Francisco. While the big bad warriors were imitating the evil culture they were commissioned to banish, a widowed immigrant shouldered the promises of God to redeem the world.

God likes to stack the deck against Himself in order to show off His grace and power, and this is what the book of Ruth is all about. While the warriors are wielding swords and worshipping idols, a famine breaks out in the land—which often happens when sin and warfare collide. So a man named Elimelech takes his wife, Naomi, and his family and flees to Moab to find food. While there, his two sons marry Moabite women, Orpah and Ruth, and settle down to start a new life.

But soon after, Elimelech and his sons die, widowing Naomi, Orpah, and Ruth. Childless widows didn't fare well in the ancient world, especially while living in a foreign land. So Naomi heads back to Israel to die in her homeland. Surprisingly, Ruth leaves her own country to follow Naomi, and like Rahab before her, she embraces Israel's God as her own (Ruth 1:16). And God's plan of redemption continues to unfold, kindled by His stubborn delight in insignificant people.

Ruth takes to the fields to find leftover grain as widows did at the time, and she finds favor in the eyes of Rahab's son Boaz—a man who wouldn't have existed were it not for God's furious love for a Canaanite harlot. Ruth and Boaz get together, and the story ends by celebrating their marriage and the birth of their firstborn son, Obed—King David's grandfather.

The story of Ruth should not be reduced to a Cinderella-like love story of a peasant who wins the heart of a prince. Neither should it be moralized. Though Ruth is a woman of excellence and seems to have a good heart, she's not exactly a perfect model for girls to follow. I would never tell my daughter to soak herself in oil and snuggle up with her half-drunk relative in a barn (Ruth 3:3–5).

Whatever Ruth and Boaz did that night is beside the point. The overarching message in the book of Ruth is all about God. His power, His wisdom, His grace, and His love for those whom society has set aside. God loves to spin salvation out of insignificant outcasts and ragamuffins (to use Brennan Manning's term), and this is why He raised up the snake-crushing King (Gen. 3:15) through a Moabite widow.

MUSICIANS AND MONSTERS

God doesn't need rippled biceps, booming stages, and cool faux hawks to build His kingdom. He uses the humble and the contrite in spirit, who tremble at His word (Isa. 66:2). And this is what God finds in Ruth's great-grandson, the shepherd boy named David.

Saul becomes Israel's first king, and he would have attracted stares in the weight room, mostly from himself. But God rejects him from being king and seeks out a man after God's own heart named David—an insignificant son of a sheepherding family. Even Samuel is shocked at God's choice. While David's brothers are out playing with swords and spears, David wanders out to the field to play his harp and write music. If David went to my high school, he would have gotten beat up.

David is courageous. But true courage, biblical courage, looks not to oneself but to the One who formed the heavens. One day, David delivers food to his brothers on the battlefield and overhears a Philistine monster mocking the Creator of the universe. David becomes infuriated. "Who is this uncircumcised Philistine, that he should defy the armies of the living God?" (1 Sam. 17:26).

We sometimes moralize this story into a tale about a boy defeating a giant. "Guess what, little Preston, *you, too*, can defeat the giants in your life." But the story of David and Goliath is fixated upon a mighty God who uses harp-playing shepherd boys to set up His unshakable kingdom on earth. This story stands in the gap between the Edenic promise of a snake-killing Son of Eve (Gen. 3) and a Jewish infant King lying in a feeding trough (Luke 2). The messianic promise has been unfolding through story after story, and its every movement has been fueled by grace. God is going to change the world through scandalous harlots, rejected widows, and harp-strumming songwriters with skinny jeans.

And it all comes to a head in the Elah Valley, as David looks through the nine-foot giant to the One who made the stars.

You come to me with a sword and with a spear and
with a javelin, but I come to you in the name of

the LORD of hosts, the God of the armies of Israel, whom you have defied. This day the LORD will deliver you into my hand, and I will strike you down and cut off your head. And I will give the dead bodies of the host of the Philistines this day to the birds of the air and to the wild beasts of the earth, that all the earth may know that there is a God in Israel, and that all this assembly may know that the LORD saves not with sword and spear. For the battle is the LORD's, and he will give you into our hand. (1 Sam. 17:45–47)

David doesn't muster up some inner strength to conquer the "giant in his life." Instead, he wants "all the earth [to] know that there is a God in Israel" and that His name is *Yahweh*. The grace that empowered Canaanite whores and foreign women is showcased here in a teenage boy with a slingshot. Nothing can stave off God's passion to use unusable people.

David runs at the giant, sinks a stone into his forehead, and chops off Goliath's head with the giant's own sword. The Philistines flee while the Israelites gloat in victory, and David goes back to the field to play his harp and write more music.

After killing Goliath, David reluctantly moves into the spotlight while Saul fades out of the picture, ultimately committing suicide on the hills of Gilboa. After a brief civil war, David emerges as the victor and king over Israel, ushering in a time of peace and righteousness. The Bible could almost end right there. God's reign over the earth is established through David, and Israel lives happily ever after. The end.

But like you and me, David is addicted to sin. And one day when he's taking an innocent stroll on his roof, he notices a beautiful woman who is also the wife of Uriah, one of David's best friends. Within seconds, the man after God's own heart turns into a man after the woman next door. David covets his neighbor's bride, has sex with her, lies about it to her husband, gets him drunk, and then kills him. If it could happen to David, it could happen to anybody. We all have it in us. That's why we all need Jesus.

FURIOUS FAVOR

I wonder if David would be allowed in our churches today. In most cases, when a church member has an affair, he is shunned at best or mistreated at worst—even if he repents. But David doesn't just have an affair. He lusts, covets, fornicates, lies, and gets another man hammered. Then he tries to keep his dirty little secrets by murdering the husband of the woman he "loves." I doubt I've met anyone as sinful as David. Have you? He breaks half of the Ten Commandments in a single episode. And he doesn't repent until he's caught.

But when Nathan shoves his prophetic finger into David's chest and rebukes him, David falls to his knees and admits his guilt. And right then, at that moment, God rips open the heavens to reach down and touch David's soul with stubborn delight. God eagerly forgives David for his sin, and all of it is buried at the bottom of the sea, never to be remembered again. There is no hiccup in God's furious favor toward David.

So why do repentant sinners still bear the stigma of "adulterer," "divorced," or "addict" in our churches today? It's one thing if they don't repent. But quite often we shun repentant sinners, like Jeffrey Dahmer, whose crimes we just can't forget. "He's the former addict." "That's the divorced mom." "Here comes the guy who slept with the church secretary." For some reason we love to define people by the sin in their lives—even *past* sin in their lives—rather than by the grace that forgave it.

It's no wonder that David pens the last sentence in Psalm 23: "Surely goodness and mercy shall [hunt me down] all the days of my life" (Ps. 23:6). This may seem like an unusual translation, but it's the literal meaning of the Hebrew word *radaph*—"to pursue, hunt, chase." *Radaph* is often translated "follow," which is terribly weak. It lacks aggression. *Radaph* is most often used in the Old Testament of a hunter chasing down his prey or of a soldier seeking to conquer his enemy. It's an aggressive word juiced up on steroids and loaded with caffeine. It describes a bloodthirsty warrior, a famished lion, a transcendent Creator who will stop at nothing until He conquers His prey. He will chase, pursue, fight, hunt with unbridled passion until He conquers and devours and loves.

God *radaphed* a lonely widow from a foreign land, a liaison for outcasts living in the slums of a depraved city, and the last-born shepherd boy who penned the words "mercy shall hunt me down," even though I had sex with my friend's wife before I murdered him. God's plan of salvation was not upheld by the mighty arms of Israel's judges, but by God's tender grip of grace on social rejects.

Looks like Jesus read His Bible growing up.

6

WHORE

SEX AND SALVATION

The Bible is stuffed full of stories about prostitutes or sexually promiscuous women. Some are depicted as objects of God's judgment: Jezebel, Delilah, and the proverbial whore of Proverbs 6 come to mind. Most female fornicators in the Bible, however, are depicted as trophies of *charis*—objects of God's shameless delight.

We've seen God take Tamar's sexual scam and turn it into a conduit of salvation in Genesis 38. He did the same with Rahab. The nation of Israel, in fact, is often compared to a promiscuous woman who has slept with every guy in the neighborhood, and this analogy most often occurs in passages where grace is the main point.[1]

It's no wonder that throughout Jesus's short ministry on earth, many prostitutes and whores encountered God's grace. In Luke 7, a religious leader condemns a prostitute, while Jesus forgives her. In John 8, Jesus rescues a woman caught in adultery from being stoned to death by a bunch of religious hypocrites and forgives her. And Jesus tells Israel's spiritual leaders that "prostitutes go into the kingdom of God before you" (Matt. 21:31). The Bible certainly doesn't approve of sexual immorality or prostitution, but in line with the dictum that God loves the sinner and hates the sin, God finds great pleasure in extending grace to sexually immoral people.

There's just something about prostitution that makes it a powerful backdrop for grace. Many streams of sin, pain, loneliness, and guilt collide when a woman rents out her body for sex with a man she'll never see again. Or maybe she will. Prostitution is the epitome of depravity and the pinnacle of pain.

My view of prostitution was reshaped after hearing the testimony of Carol,[2] a streetwalker from the slums of Springfield, Ohio, who converted to Christ. "I didn't wake up one day and decide to be a prostitute," she told me. "I had a job, a house, a family. *I was living the same life you are.*" But after Carol's husband left her, she lost her house, her family, and her job, and she ended up coddling a bottle of whiskey—the only hope she had left. But drinking led to drugs, and drugs led to more drugs. Before she knew it, Carol was on the streets, scrambling to support her habit. And the streets are a frightening place when you're a woman in need of food, shelter, and rivers of heroin.

"Work for me and I'll protect you, provide for you, and keep a steady flow of heroin pumping through your veins," promised a pimp. And the rest is history. Carol was a sinner engaged in sinful activity—aren't we all?—but a complex web of personal sin and societal evil nurtured her downward spiral into prostitution.

One thing Carol told me still haunts me to this day and forces me on my knees, begging for more grace. She said, "We are all one bad decision away from being on the streets."

Really? All of us? One bad decision?

Yes. She is absolutely correct.

One bad decision. All of us. Really.

At the height of his morality, King David plummeted to the valley of wickedness, and it began with one bad decision. Sin, pain, loneliness, and twisted sexual sins are crouching at our door waiting to pounce on us. Yet we—through the power and grace of God—must master them. We would all be streetwalkers were it not for the grace of God. Awana champions and soccer moms included.

EZEKIEL 16 REMIXED

Of all the stories of whores in the Bible, Ezekiel 16 is the most daring. Like Genesis 38, this chapter must have slipped past the angelic editors when God decided to put it into His Holy Book. Ezekiel 16 is a lengthy allegory (think extended metaphor, like *The Chronicles of Narnia*) of grace that pushes the limits of holy language. One evangelical commentator says that Ezekiel 16 is "semipornographic," and he's right.[3] *Porno* comes from *porneia*, which means "fornication," and *graphic* comes from *grapho*, which means "to write." Ezekiel 16 writes about fornication; it's—literally—divinely inspired pornography. Were it put to film, this chapter would be X-rated. No question. But unlike the filthy stuff produced in the pornography studios of Los Angeles, Ezekiel 16 is designed to rebuke sin, not encourage it. The offensive language that Ezekiel uses is intended to shock the Israelites out of their complacency and send a wake-up call shivering up their spines. It certainly did to mine the first time I read it. It's one thing to say, "You're a sinner. Stop it!" but quite another to say, "You became a common whore, grabbing anyone coming down the street and taking him into your bed" (Ezek. 16:15 MSG).

Most of all, Ezekiel 16 is a stunning portrait of grace. Inasmuch as the Israelites resemble human nature as a whole, this allegory reveals God's love for you and me. So let's read Ezekiel 16 as if it were our autobiography. In many ways it is. But in order to get inside the story and make it our own, we'll have to contemporize it a bit. So here's the allegory of Ezekiel 16—remixed.

Your father was a pimp and your mother was a prostitute. Your mom found a lucrative way to fund her drug habit by having sex with multiple men, until your father took her in (and a few others) to live under his roof. When a pimp lives with a prostitute, one thing leads to another, and that's where you came in. With the help of some crack and a bottle of Jack, you were conceived and immediately unwanted. Too scared to have an abortion, your mother waited until you were born, then casually dumped you—her newborn daughter—in a nearby garbage can.

Minutes later, a stranger walked by and heard the squalling from inside the bin. He opened the lid and found you—squirming in your blood, expelling your last breath of life. The stranger's 911 call miraculously summoned an ambulance within minutes, and you were saved.

But still unwanted.

The stranger couldn't bear the thought of sending you to a foster home, so he signed some papers and took you into his home. But "home" is an understatement. Your new father was the CEO of a multimillion-dollar business. Your new home was a small castle, and your future life would be paradisiacal.

And he was a good man too. Humble, strong, generous, and honest. Your new father possessed an unusual joy, which he never failed to shower on you. His time, his money, his affection, his attention—they were all yours. There was nothing you lacked. All the storybook tales combined could not compare to your utopian life. You were the envy of all your friends and the prized possession of a father who had it all. From his perspective, though, "having it all" meant having you. You were the source of his uncanny joy.

But something snapped when you turned sixteen. The boys at school started noticing your body and didn't hide their stares. Stares turned to comments. Comments turned to caresses. And caresses opened the floodgates of a different kind of love—one that was both exhilarating and empty, but too addicting to resist.

So at the age of sixteen, you moved out of your father's house, leaving him in pools of tears. You didn't hide the fact that you were happily leaving him in order to fornicate with your new boyfriend. The more he wept, the more you laughed, as you skidded off in your boyfriend's Camaro.

Your adolescent love affair was only the beginning. Before long, your boyfriend's buddies took a liking to you, and the flirtatious cycle was revisited. Soon, mere sex with your boyfriend became boring, so his friends were added to the mix. But even orgies became dull over time, and drugs, alcohol, and other men—older and creepier—joined in the hellish dance. Your dream of freedom and love had turned into a nightmare.

But nothing can compare to the pain of the day when your boyfriend decided to mail a picture of you to your father's house. Delighted to catch a glimpse of his princess, your father laid his eyes upon a sullied whore. Your once silky hair was frayed and knotted. Your eyes—the windows to your soul—were dark and sunken. Devoid of life. And the bruises on your face revealed that your boyfriend's love had run dry. Daddy's baby girl was the not-so-prized possession of half a dozen drug-infused teenagers. And there was nothing he could do.

Sex, drugs, and imaginative acts of depravity piled up as you lived the next two years satisfying your misguided lust for life on nameless boys who used and abused you. Yet you still used them to satisfy your craving to be loved. You gave one boy the car Daddy bought you on your sweet sixteen. Your boyfriend's other girlfriend took the dress your father made. And you sold the necklace that belonged to your grandmother to buy heroin for another man. Yet the beatings continued. Soon your bank account ran out, and you took to the streets to sell your body in order to keep a steady flow of heroin pumping through your veins.

And heaven began to rumble with furious excitement.

Now, you're sitting in your room. Your "friends" are gone and you are all alone. Coming down off a high, you begin to feel depressed and lonely; your humanity is slipping away. So you head for another hit to numb the pain. Just then, someone kicks open the door and a burst of fear squeezes your heart. The bruises on your body are tender reminders that your new home is never safe. Kicked-in doors are a regular occurrence, and they lead only to pain. Or sex. Both, actually.

The fear runs deep. Maybe it's the suddenness of the blast. Or maybe you just need to feed your starving addiction. Your pale stare quickly changes as you see the man standing at the threshold. It's your father.

Your fear intensifies. You recall the day you sped away from his house laughing as he stood on his lawn weeping. How did he find you? Why has he come? Is he, too, going to beat you after all you've done?

His tears speak otherwise. His face glistens with joy. His hands tremble. You can hear his heart thump through his chest. Tears cascade down his cheeks, but now they look different. These are tears of adoration and triumph. And they are flowing because your daddy has found his baby girl. The one who found you wailing in a Dumpster has once again taken the initiative to redeem you and enjoy you again.

Confused, enthralled, terrified, overjoyed—you can't move.

But your father can. He races across the room to swallow you with an embrace—the first nonsexual touch you have felt in years. A touch that radiates more love than all your sexual encounters put together. You finally feel safe. Loved. Forgiven instantly, as your dad gathers your face in his hands and declares:

> I'll restore the relationship we had when you were young, only this time it will be better. It will last forever, and nothing will lure you away from me again. You'll remember your past life and face the shame of it, but when I shower you with the good life you had as before, it will make your shame fade from your memory. Don't try to fix it. I'll fix it for you. I'll make everything right after all you've done, and it will leave you speechless. (Ezek. 16:60–63, modified from MSG)

Grace. This stuff never gets old.

HOMESCHOOLED WHORE

We were all wayward whores. If you're a homeschooling mom, missionary kid, pastor, or drug dealer, you were a whore loved by God. Or in Ezekiel's words:

> You took all that fine jewelry I gave you, my gold and my silver, and made pornographic images of them for your brothels. (16:17 MSG)

> You took your sons and your daughters, whom you had given birth to as my children, and you killed them, sacrificing them to idols. Wasn't it bad enough that you had become a whore? And now you're a murderer, killing my children and sacrificing them to idols. (16:20–21 MSG)

> Not once during these years of outrageous obscenities and whorings did you remember your infancy, when you were naked and exposed, a blood-smeared newborn. (16:22 MSG)

> At every major intersection you built your bold brothels and exposed your sluttish sex, spreading

your legs for everyone who passed by. (16:24 MSG)

You went international with your whoring. You fornicated with the Egyptians, seeking them out in their sex orgies. (16:25–26 MSG)

Even the Philistine women—can you believe it?— were shocked at your sluttish life. (16:27 MSG)

What a sick soul! Doing all this stuff—the champion whore! You built your bold brothels at every major intersection, opened up your whorehouses in every neighborhood, but you were different from regular whores in that you wouldn't accept a fee. (16:30–31 MSG)

You bribe men from all over to come to bed with you! You're just the opposite of the regular whores who get paid for sex. Instead, you pay men for their favors! You even pervert whoredom! (16:33–34 MSG)

Whatever your actual autobiography looks like, Ezekiel 16 is your spiritual autobiography. You were a promiscuous sinner delightfully forgiven by Jesus—the One who found you in the Dumpster and turned you into a real ingredient of divine happiness.

Some of you reading this book are still on your prodigal journey, and you think your mess is keeping you from Jesus. "If I went to church, a bolt of lightning would strike the building," I often hear people say. You feel guilty, discouraged, and unlovable; yet you're unable to shake your addiction to boys, girls, porn, drugs, friends, fame, starving yourself, or cutting your body. You think you need to clean yourself up *so that* Jesus will love you. But you've put the cart before the horse. Ezekiel 16 offensively proclaims that God takes the initiative to love us and redeem us. God pursues wayward whores with His unconditional, one-way love *so that* He can clean us up. He won't send a bolt of lightning to take care of your sin. He already sent a Son.

Such unilateral love saturates the Old Testament, especially the prophets. Ezekiel 16 paints an allegory to drive this home, while the book of Hosea gives an autobiography of a holy man who lives this stuff out. It's one thing to write a story about grace and quite another to embody grace by marrying a slut.

HALF-PRICED WHORE

Try to throw a leash on grace, and the book of Hosea will snap it. The grace of Hosea doesn't settle down. It cannot be domesticated. Hosea's *charis* wears leather and rides a Harley. If you want to read this book in Sunday school, you'll have to first neuter it. Hosea's *charis* is gasoline set next to an open flame, Bono performing live in Dublin.

God commands Hosea to live out the allegory of Ezekiel 16: "Go, take to yourself a wife of whoredom," God says, "and have children of whoredom" (Hosea 1:2).[4] The book doesn't record Hosea's response, but I'm sure it was outrage. "But, God, I'm a prophet. I'm a pastor. I'm a holy man. This woman's going to destroy my testimony. How's my wife going to lead Beth Moore studies when she's a whore?"

But God's not interested in Hosea's reputation. He's singularly focused on branding Hosea's soul with the scandal of divine *charis*. "Go marry a whore, Hosea. Love the unlovable. Then you will experience what it's like to be on the divine side of unconditional grace."

Grace will not be a Christianese buzzword for Hosea.

So Hosea finds a village woman named Gomer who's known for being the town whore. Hosea asks for her hand in marriage, and for some unknown reason, she says yes.

We're not told much about their marriage, but they have at least three children. The next time we see Gomer is in chapter 3, but something has changed. She's no longer married to Hosea. In fact, she's no longer married to anyone. In chapter 3, Gomer—the town slut—is now up for sale.

> The LORD said to me, "Go again, love a woman who is loved by another man and is an adulteress, even as the LORD loves the children of Israel, though they turn to other gods...." So I bought her for fifteen shekels of silver and [nine bushels] of barley. (3:1–2)

Gomer is not named, but the context shows that this is the same woman. We're not sure when or why Gomer left Hosea after their wedding, but it's clear they are not together anymore since she's now up for sale—most likely being sold as a slave.

Perhaps her life as a promiscuous woman was so etched into her bones that having sex with multiple men had taken over her identity. And although she hated it, she couldn't escape it. So one day she decided to leave Hosea to go back to her old way of life—sleeping around with whomever was willing and able. After she bounced from man to man, one of these men finally got sick of it and sold her into slavery—not an uncommon thing in that day. And now in Hosea 3, we find Gomer standing among various other women being sold at a local slave market.

Slaves were bought for various reasons: to help out on the farm or for assistance in raising the kids at home. Female slaves were often used for sexual services. But Gomer is not a very valuable product among the lineup of slaves. We know this because the price that Hosea ends up paying for Gomer is only fifteen shekels and a bunch of barley. This was only half the price of the average female slave at that time.

We don't know why her price is so low, but it probably means that she is not looked upon as having much value among her would-be buyers. Maybe her physical appearance is repulsive. Her clothes are probably filled with the stench of a rotting lifestyle. Her hair perhaps is unkempt and weathered. Her body may be unfit, diseased, scarred, or just plain unable to fulfill the physical duties of a domestic slave or to act out the sexual fantasies of the hungry men looking on with blank stares and hollow souls.

Gomer has nothing going for her, and her price tag publicly proves this.

One by one, the other more beautiful, more physically appealing women are bought for a high price. The shame of being passed over as a worthless product is probably nothing new to Gomer. Aside from the distant, hazy memory of her marriage to Hosea, she can't remember what it feels like to be valued in the eyes of another. But then she hears a familiar voice:

"I'll take her. No, not that one. The other one. The one in the back row."

Gomer hears the onlooking crowd snicker and laugh.

"No, not that one," yells the bidder, "the one behind her. Yes, the one with the muddy dress."

The onlookers begin to laugh even harder, shaking their heads in disbelief. They realize that the man is bidding on Gomer.

Gomer?

The half-priced whore? The shamed woman who has no value?

Gomer looks out past her crusty, stench-filled hair and sees a face from the distant past: *Hosea.* The man who found her on the streets and married her. The man who endured five or six or seven affairs (Gomer lost track after the fourth). The man who kept pursuing her and loving her—who was genuinely heartbroken when she began sleeping around—is seeking to buy her back.

"Buy me back? Buy *me* back?"

"Yes, yes, I know who it is," hollers Hosea. "I want her. I'll pay any price for her! I love her and I want to be with her! I want to remarry her and be committed to her *because I delight in her.*"

The whole crowd now is doubled over in laughter and disbelief. One persistent villager can't let such disgrace continue, so he rebukes Hosea.

"Get a grip, Hosea! You're embarrassing yourself! That's the woman who has slept with half the guys in this village! She's made a mockery of you. She's shamed you beyond what any guy could endure. She didn't even want to be with you then. And look at her now!"

But Hosea fights his way through the crowd and cries out, "I don't care what she looks like! I don't care what she's done! And I don't care what she has become! I know she didn't love me as much as I loved her, and I know that she has a lustful addiction for having sex with other men. But I love her. And I will never stop loving her. That's … my … wife! Get out of my way and *give me my bride.* I'll pay any price."

Hosea's scandalous, shameless, one-way love for his unlovable whore is a mere snapshot of God's grace toward us. While we were still whores, Christ eagerly climbed up on the cross to redeem us from the slave market.

God loves you because of who He is and because of what Christ has done. Whether you are depressed, suicidal, underweight, overweight, good-looking, ugly, dumb, smart, popular, socially rejected, happily married, divorced, physically fit, physically disabled, funny, dull—whether you are Judah or Joseph, Gomer or a Proverbs 31 woman—you have won the heart of God because you are human. God doesn't save people who have it all together. He saves whores, prostitutes, porn stars, Bible college professors, and stay-at-home housewives who wear head coverings in church, because God loves to create righteousness out of nothing.

Grace. If this stuff ever gets old, we might as well throw away our Bibles. I never get tired of seeing tears stream down the cheeks of people like Carol when they talk about Jesus finding them on the streets. To hear former streetwalkers talk about grace and how Jesus values them despite their past is better than ten thousand church services. And I can't think of a better mirror to Jesus's pursuit of me.

We are all vile sinners, addicted to the muck and sludge of our own depravity; we are victims beaten down by other people's depravity. We are therefore walking magnets for God's scandalous grace.

We are Gomer.

7

TATTOO

CARVED BY GRACE

I don't have a tattoo, but I've always wanted one. I'm not sure why. Maybe it's the "tough guy" image every guy wants. Maybe it's the attention they garner, the messages they send, or perhaps I want to let people know that even though I go to church, I can still kick their butt.

But I'll probably never get a tattoo. For one, my wife would never have it. It's one thing if I already had a tattoo. This might actually be sexy in her eyes. ("I married a guy with a past, but now he's settled down, ooh la la.") But even if my wife did give me the green light to brand my body, I still don't think I would for one reason that's hard to get around. Tattoos are permanent. What if I change my mind? What if I don't like it any longer? What if I gain weight and stretch my Christian ichthus into a blowfish? The idea of permanency scares me.

But God is all about permanency. We know this because God has a tattoo and it's got our names on it.

> Behold, I have engraved you on the palms of my hands. (Isa. 49:16)

Tattoos were quite common in the ancient world. People got tattoos for different reasons. Egyptian women tattooed their stomachs and breasts during pregnancy to ensure a safe birth. Slaves in other cultures got tattoos to identify them as the property of another. Criminals were sometimes forced to get a tattoo to bear the stigma of their crime. The Greeks and Romans got a tattoo to show allegiance to their god. For instance, King Ptolemy IV, who ruled a Greek-speaking empire that included Egypt from 221 to 205 BC, tattooed his body with ivy leaves to show his devotion to Dionysus, the god of wine.[1] Sounds like something that would happen at a frat party. I'm sure it has.

God's tattoo is probably similar to Ptolemy's, only God turns the meaning on its head. While Ptolemy and other kings were running around, flaunting their devotion to their god—*"I'm devoted to Dionysus; I'm devoted to Dionysus!"*—your God sits on His throne and declares, "I'm devoted to *you*! And I've put my palms under the needle to prove it."

God is so committed to you that He has carved your name into the palms of His hands. Our God is not afraid of permanency.

GRACE: FROM DAVID TO EXILE

This image of God's tattoo becomes even more powerful when we understand the spiritual state of God's people when Isaiah 49 was written. After David dies, Israel's kingdom begins to deteriorate. Solomon, the successor to David's throne, ends up ruling with a heavy hand. Though he acquires much luxury and wealth, he hoards it for himself while Israel lives in grinding poverty. Morally speaking, Solomon is a mess. Though he "loves God," he also worships idols and has an insatiable thirst for pagan women. Lots of them. The Bible offers a scathing review of Solomon's life (1 Kings 11).

But God is committed to David's snake-killing genealogical line. And God's unswerving commitment forms the backbone to Israel's kingdom. Kings come and go, but God's promise stands firm. Most of the kings are evil and lead Israel into wickedness. Abijam marries fourteen different women. Ahaz worships the gods of Assyria and commits spiritual whoredom, according to the prophets. Rehoboam sets up cultic shrines to foreign gods where male prostitutes can have sex with other men (or women) in order to compel foreign gods to shower their semen—that is, rain—on the crops. King Manasseh is so twisted that he burns his kids alive to show his zeal for a foreign god named Molech, who demands such things. Jeffrey Dahmer would fit right in, though the tenants of the Boyd would be pretty creeped out. Though there are a few good kings mixed in, these are dark days in Israel.

And it isn't just the kings who are wicked. The entire nation is weighed down with evil hearts that enjoy fornication, idolatry, murder, oppression, theft, and volunteering for service at Rehoboam's brothels. God's people are so given to evil that the prophets compare Israel's sinfulness to the spots of a leopard etched into its fur, or a donkey in heat that wants to hump anything on four legs, or a valley of dry, dusty skeletons.[2]

PROPHETS OF DOOM AND GLOOM AND GRACE

The prophet Isaiah is also quite graphic in describing Israel's degenerate state. He reaches deep for imaginative metaphors to drive this home.

How the faithful city
>   has become a whore. (1:21)

You have burdened me with your sins;
>   you have wearied me with your iniquities.
>>   (43:24)

But you ... sons of the sorceress,
>   offspring of the adulterer and the loose
>>   woman. (57:3)

You who burn with lust among the oaks,
>   under every green tree,
who slaughter your children in the valleys. (57:5)

Their feet run to evil,
>   and they are swift to shed innocent blood. (59:7)

When God gets around to affirming Israel's "righteousness," He compares it to a bloody menstrual rag (Isa. 64:6).

But even though Israel is unlovable, unusable, unworthy of anything but wrath, she is still the people upon whom the Creator God set His affection. In the words of Augustine, the church is a whore but she's my mother. God would say Israel is a whore but she's my bride. In fact, this is exactly what God says in several prophetic books, as we have seen. For now, let's come back to God's tattoo.

Isaiah 49:16 says that God has Israel's name tattooed on the palms of His hands. Here's the vital point: God's commitment to Israel is not and simply *cannot* be based on any good it has done.

God doesn't look at Israel's used menstrual rag and say, "Hey, now there's something that's beautiful; I'm going to reward them for that." The same people He calls a whore are etched into the palms of His hands. The one who is swift toward evil is hunted down by a Creator who delights in conquering sinners with boundless grace. God hates the sin but loves the sinner—a statement that's more profound than we sometimes realize. And He's tattooed their names on His hands to prove it.

Still think God loves you because you do your devotions?

God loves you because of God. And God's tattoo is only one of many metaphors that the prophet Isaiah uses to convey his message of unilateral grace. The book of Isaiah radiates with the stunning beauty of grace like a ray of light refracted through a priceless jewel. Meditate on this book. Read it often. Memorize its verses. Explore the rich images that the prophet paints in order to soak us in God's unconditional love for unlovable people. Do this, and you will have a tough time banking on your own morality to sustain God's love for you.

PRONE TO PURSUE

Here's God's response to Israel, as she lies intoxicated with her own lust for evil:

> Therefore the LORD waits to be gracious to you,
>   and therefore he [lifts himself up] to show
>   mercy to you.

> For the LORD is a God of justice;
>> blessed are all those who wait for him. (Isa. 30:18)[3]

Since Israel is unwilling to turn to God (Isa. 30:15), God turns to Israel. But this isn't a coldhearted, impatient, "fine, I'll save you" sort of turning. Isaiah says that God is eagerly longing to bring Israel back to Himself. God is lifting Himself up, or standing on His tiptoes, with a fervent longing to restore His relationship with His people.

> And your ears shall hear a word behind you, saying,
> "This is the way, walk in it," when you turn to the
> right or when you turn to the left. (Isa. 30:21)

This isn't the image of a taskmaster, an angry father waiting to spank you when you mess up. God is depicted here as a Teacher, a Guide, One who walks with you as you walk with Him. He tenderly coaches you in your obedience and is intimately involved in your repentance. This is the "word behind you" that helps you walk in righteousness. Therefore, there is no reason to fear:

> Fear not, for I am with you;
>> be not dismayed, for I am your God;
> I will strengthen you, I will help you,
>> I will uphold you with my righteous right hand....
> I, the LORD your God,
>> hold your right hand;
> it is I who say to you, "Fear not,
>> I am the one who helps you....

> Fear not, for I have redeemed you;
>> I have called you by name, you are mine....
> Because you are precious in my eyes,
>> and honored, and I love you....
> Fear not, for I am with you." (Isa. 41:10, 13; 43:1, 4, 5)

We are precious in God's eyes; we are loved by our Creator; we are honored, helped, and comforted by our King not because of what we do, but because of who He is. Not because of what we've done, but because of what He has done. We are prone to wander; God is prone to pursue:

> You did not call upon me, O Jacob;
>> but you have been weary of me, O Israel! ...
> You have burdened me with your sins;
>> you have wearied me with your iniquities. (Isa.
>>> 43:22, 24)

Israel hasn't called upon God. Israel is weary of God. But where we expect judgment, God responds with grace:

> I, I am he
>> who blots out your transgressions for my own
>> sake,
>> and I will not remember your sins. (Isa. 43:25)

No one is twisting God's arm to cut us some slack, to show a little leniency. Grace is not leniency. Grace is what compels God to act on His own initiative for His own glory to do what no other god can do: forgive those who don't deserve it and cannot earn it. God is holy and intimate, and *therefore* He delights in forgiving unforgivable people.

> You shall be a crown of beauty in the hand of the
>   Lord,
>   and a royal diadem in the hand of your
>   God....
> You shall be called My Delight Is in Her ...
>   for the Lord delights in you....
> As the bridegroom rejoices over the bride,
>   so shall your God rejoice over you. (Isa.
>   62:3–5)

I love that last line. "As the bridegroom rejoices over the bride, so shall your God rejoice over you." On one level or another, we all desire to be loved—to be considered beautiful in the eyes of another. Girls wear nice clothes that accentuate their bodies or hide any defects they think they have. They put on makeup, perfume, and lotion to make their appearance more appealing. Guys go to the gym, buy a car they can't afford, and advertise their success to garner attention.

We are a generation of lovers who long to be loved. We spend exorbitant amounts of money to compel others to delight in us. We construct our ideal life on Facebook because we are unsatisfied with our real life, which is tainted with boredom, loneliness, insecurity, and a lack of friends and followers. We do not enjoy the person God created us to be or the life God has gifted us with. We think we are overweight, underweight, too pale, too dark, too plain, or just plain boring. Yet we crave to be delighted in by a significant other. So we pursue misguided avenues to make ourselves delightful, to satisfy our craving to be loved.

Such was the case of Zach, my friend and former student.

PLASTIC CHRISTIANS

I was a new professor at a conservative evangelical university, where all the students are perfect—or so they seem. Zach looked like everyone else at the school. He was clean-cut, well dressed, and had memorized all the Christian lingo that we use to convince others of our spirituality. Zach was physically fit, confident, and knew his Bible well.

One day, Zach wanted to go to coffee to share his story with me. My view of Zach—and many other students—would never be the same. Zach told me that he grew up in a Christian home and went to church most of his life. But one thing set Zach apart from other kids at his church. Zach was gay.

Behind the plastic smile and perfect hair was a pile of pain. Zach told me that he never had a deep-seated desire to be with other men growing up. He only desired to be loved. But he had certain character traits that typify homosexuals, and so his friends—churchgoing friends—mocked and shunned him. Like all people, Zach desired relationship. He desired to be delighted in as a bridegroom delights in his bride. One day when he was eighteen, the eyes of another man affectionately gazed upon Zach and flooded his heart with significance. Whatever homosexual impulse lay dormant in Zach was ignited by the gift of value given by another human.

So Zach entered into a homosexual lifestyle.

"I was never happy as a homosexual," Zach told me. "It was only a means of covering up my deep pain of feeling unloved and insignificant."

"Really?" I asked. "You were never happy?"

"I wasn't," Zach said confidently. "I had a deep desire to be loved. I craved value. And my Christian friends never mediated God's value to me."

Zach's experience with homosexuality can't speak for every person who is attracted to the same sex. But he did say that many others shared his feelings. "Every homosexual I knew had a similar pain of feeling unloved, and same-sex relationships were one way to numb it."

I can't verify Zach's assessment, and as a straight man, I could never make such claims. Homosexuality is a very complicated issue that we can't get into here. But even if there is only some truth to his opinion, then Isaiah's words are all the more relevant. The Creator of the universe delights in you as a bridegroom delights in his bride.

Zach had left his homosexual lifestyle about a year before I met him. He did not believe it was morally right, nor did he believe it was his natural orientation. At least for Zach, his same-sex attraction was unwanted.

One day, during a school chapel where students shared their testimonies, Zach stood up and told his story to three thousand college students. Trembling as he read his script, Zach shared about his homosexual past and how he had recently found his identity in

Christ—the true source of value and worth. After he finished, the place was silent. Scared of how people would respond, especially the guys, Zach stood there—vulnerable, relieved, frightened, insecure. Almost instantly, a dozen or so college guys jumped up to embrace Zach with nonhomoerotic affection. Zach felt the love of Jesus as he's never experienced it before. The body of Christ mediated the Creator's delight in Zach. And the chapel flowed with tears worthy of Eden.

Zach and I downed a lot of coffee together that year. Once a week we would get together to chat about life and the remaining struggles that he had. "You know, Preston, there's a lot of people here who struggle with unwanted homosexual feelings. Some, in fact, don't struggle. They're actively engaged in homosexual relationships." Such is common on a college campus. But remember, this was a conservative evangelical university. The students had a dress code and a curfew, and they couldn't drink alcohol, even if they were twenty-one. Yet many of them—these clean-cut, well-dressed Awana champions, who grew up in conservative homes, knew all the Christian lingo, and memorized whole books of the Bible—engaged in homoerotic love.

CUTTING, STARVING, STRANGLING

I used to look out at the beautiful faces in my classes with confidence that they were doing just fine—nice hair, plastic faces. But after meeting Zach, I look at them differently. I now see a bunch of Gomers and Tamars, Judahs and Davids, seeking to alleviate some excruciating pain in their lives. I see men and women scarred by the harm they have suffered and the harm they do. I see broken but beautiful objects of God's shameless delight.

Young Christians everywhere are crying out silently for someone to soothe their pain, to show them value, to delight in them as a bridegroom sings over his bride.

According to one poll, 41 percent of Christians either have engaged in some form of self-mutilation or know of someone who has.[4] The practice is especially common among teenagers. They slash their bodies with razor blades not to commit suicide but as a way of redirecting the pain that's caving in on their soul. *I hate myself, I'm so ugly,* or *I want someone to care about me* are the thoughts these image bearers have prior to mutilating their bodies.[5] "I love God with all my heart. But I feel so trapped," one teenage girl reported. And so she used her stomach as a "billboard," as she called it, to carve words of pain she couldn't tell anyone else.[6]

Nearly one-third of all college students struggle with an eating disorder, such as binge eating, self-induced vomiting, or unhealthy weight loss. Hardly any of them are actually obese. They simply fall short of some false standard of perfection fed to them by our culture, their parents, or the church.

Laurie struggled with bulimia nervosa ever since she was thirteen, and it was brought on not by her self-perception but by comments made by her classmates and parents. "Church is not always a grace-filled place, especially where I grew up," Laurie recalls. "It focused on actions—telling us we could make ourselves pure by doing the right things.... I was obsessed with being perfect, but I had a lot of anger because I wasn't perfect. I turned to food to placate myself and feel happy."[7] So Laurie began starving herself in the hope of feeding her desire for love. But the starving led to anger, anger led to isolation, and isolation led to clinical depression, until one day she tried to strangle herself. "No one at church knew how to respond to me," Laurie says. "People were freaked out by my depression but didn't know how to deal with it. I felt so alone."

The good news is that Laurie stopped short of strangling herself. "Everything that happened was under the umbrella of God's grace; I see that now," Laurie says. "When I started understanding how He sees me and how He loves me, it was a big, freeing step for me."[8]

Laurie caught a glimpse of God's tattoo.

Why are these conservative Christians, who look and sound good on the outside, rotting away with unspeakable pain? What would drive them to starve themselves to win someone's affection, pursue homosexual love to satisfy a desire to be loved, or slash their own bodies to feel momentary relief from an out-of-control life? Laurie hit the nail on the head.

What's missing is grace.

Grace. Not the doctrine. Not the buzzword. But shameless, unconditional *charis* pulled down from heaven and embodied in the hands and feet of God's people. *Charis*: the life-giving relationship with a lonely outcast on the verge of suicide.

GRACE EMBODIED

I emphasize grace embodied because the Lauries around us struggle to believe in *charis*, not because the Bible is hard to understand, but because too often the message they experience from people over-whelms the message God wants their hearts to hear.

About one out of every four college students has been sexually abused growing up.[9] Unfortunately, students from Christian homes are not exempt. I discovered this is why many freshmen don't look forward to going home during Thanksgiving break. They know they'll have to revisit—and possibly endure—the abuse they grew up with, some by the hands of churchgoing parents. These same students end up turning to porn, drugs, sex, cutting, or isolation, too scared to risk a relationship with other students. It's no wonder that nearly half of college students experience depression,[10] and suicide is now the leading cause of death among the same.[11]

A woman I'll call Andrea told me this:

> I grew up going to church, but by the time I reached high school I had lost hope that God was real. My parents fought a lot, and my dad slept around. At age eleven I sought safety and comfort from another male relative, and that went very wrong. I lost my virginity against my will.
>
> Then a guy at school told me this passionate story about his faith in Jesus. He seemed really different, a good guy. I bought in. I prayed the prayer, memorized the verses, started reading my Bible daily. We went to church and youth group every week. It helped me a lot until the night the youth leader talked about how important it is to keep your virginity. He said losing it is a sin, and

once you lose it, that's it. I had lost mine as a kid. I walked out of that room knowing I had blown it for good. "Once you lose it, that's it."

These were good Christian people, but it was a long time before anybody helped me pull apart the tangled knots of the sins done to me and the sins I did in response. Losing your virginity at eleven is somebody else's sin, not yours. God doesn't offer you the grace of forgiveness for that, because He doesn't hold you responsible. He offers you the grace of healing.

The sins I have committed in response to abuse, on the other hand, are all mine. Like doing the same things to please my Christian boyfriend that I had done for the male relative. Those sins are mine, and for those I'm grateful every day for the grace of forgiveness.

What does *charis* look like for a person like Andrea? It comes in the word preached, yes, telling us that God pursues us to restore whatever we lost at whatever age, whether by our own sin or someone else's. The word that calls us depraved for what we do, not for what is done to us. It also comes, crucially, in the word lived: the nonerotic embrace of friendship, the afternoon spent listening to an anguished story, the ongoing warmth of relationship that tells the victim she's no more a whore than we are.

Jesus came into our world as a man to embody grace. He left us, the church, to be the body of Christ, not a flock of parakeets that repeat Christian jargon but the ongoing in-the-flesh presence of His grace. We are the evidence that God's grace is more than just words.

STARVING FOR GRACE

Cutting, starving, strangling, fornicating. These are all misguided ways of satisfying our craving to be loved—to be viewed as a royal diadem by somebody else. These sufferers haven't experienced the Creator's delight in them. Grace got lost somewhere between heaven and earth. But despite the confusion, despite the pain, despite the many questions that may never receive a soothing answer, our Creator rejoices as a bridegroom over His bride, and He's got a tattoo with our name written on it.

It's not that grace will take away the struggle. People are born, I believe, with all sorts of innate addictions to self, power, and greed, and many have an insatiable desire for homoerotic (or heteroerotic) sex. And grace doesn't always take away the pain of an abuse victim. These manifold struggles will continue until Christ returns. But lack of grace combined with performance-driven spirituality forces us to spackle over our struggles with the thin veneer of Christianese rhetoric.

Life in a fallen world will breed pain. It's inevitable. It's expected. But there's no reason for us to hide this pain so no one can see it. If the kid growing up in a conservative evangelical home who experiences same-sex attraction was confident that her name was tattooed on the palms of God's hands (and her parents and church were confident of this too), then she could tap into the rich, healing powers of grace. She (or he) should never feel alone, unloved, or any more guilty than the rest of us Judahs and Gomers.

But whenever the church fails to mediate God's counterintuitive delight in broken people, the pain of sin will only be magnified until it suffocates our souls. Good deeds and spiritual lingo can't heal a human heart suffocated by evil. Only grace can. Rich, embodied, earthy *charis*. And if God tattooed on His hands the names of the male cult prostitutes in Israel (and according to Isaiah 49:16, He did), then God has your name etched into His being as well, regardless of how dark you think your struggle may be. Because God looks upon us as radiant brides—even though we're whores.

8

MANGER

GRACE UNDER A BRIDGE

America has no shortage of megachurches that glimmer with stage lights and thunder with deafening sound systems. But one of my favorite churches doesn't have any lights. No building, no stage, no bells and whistles—it doesn't even have a paid pastor. In fact, this particular church meets under an overpass off I-35 and Fourth Street in Waco, Texas. The Church Under the Bridge, as it's aptly called, is a powerful portrait of the incarnation—God taking on flesh.

In 1992, Jimmy and Janet Dorrell left the suburbs to reach out to several homeless people living under an overpass. They began by leading Bible studies and caring for practical needs, and as the gatherings grew, the Dorrells ended up starting a church. But they didn't hustle everyone back to the suburbs where churches belong. They stayed right there where the people were, right there under the bridge.

Today, hundreds of the most diverse people you could imagine gather every Sunday to worship Jesus. Recovering addicts, college students, affluent businesspeople, homeless mothers, and truckers who just drove over the church all gather in unison to celebrate Jesus's victory over their sin. "An ordinary church made holy by

His presence" is their motto, and it could not be more theologically sound. Cigarette smoke and cheap perfume waft through the air, purified by a thick aura of grace—all because one suburban couple decided to incarnate.

GRACE IN A FEEDING TROUGH

God also left His cosmic suburb to meet us under a bridge:

> And Joseph also went up from Galilee, from the town of Nazareth, to Judea, to the city of David, which is called Bethlehem, because he was of the house and lineage of David, to be registered with Mary, his betrothed, who was with child. And while they were there, the time came for her to give birth. And she gave birth to her firstborn son and wrapped him in swaddling cloths and laid him in a manger, because there was no place for them in the inn. (Luke 2:4–7)

We're so familiar with the story that we hardly notice its scandal. But think about the scenario. Mary was found pregnant out of wedlock in a culture where such shameful deeds were intolerable, and her "Holy Ghost" story would only intensify the ridicule. What would you say if your daughter or sister or girlfriend or wife came to you with such a tale? "No, really, it was God who did this. I'm telling the truth. See, I had this vision …" Yeah right.

Instead of stoning his fiancée, Joseph decided to divorce her.[1] But God stopped him in his tracks and convinced him that Mary's Holy Ghost story was actually true. So Mary and Joseph endured the shame together once Mary's belly expanded into evidence.

Luckily, Rome called for a census, which required the couple to leave Nazareth and travel to Joseph's village of origin: Bethlehem. The rugged journey provided a soothing respite from public shame, no doubt. But once they entered Bethlehem, more judgmental eyebrows were raised and the scandal continued.

Popular renditions of the Christmas story reflect little historical truth. Jesus was most likely not born outside of a commercial "inn," as our English translations suggest (Luke 2:7). The word *kataluma* can refer to an ancient motel, but it usually refers to a spare room of a house, not an "inn." There probably weren't any commercial inns in a small village like Bethlehem, so "spare room" is the best translation of the word *kataluma*.[2] So when Mary and Joseph sought shelter in their hometown of Bethlehem, they almost certainly went to a house of a relative and asked to stay in his spare room, his *kataluma*.

"Sorry," the relative said, eyeing Mary's expanded waistline. "There's no space in our *kataluma*. You'll have to sleep out with the animals."

"But, sir," Joseph pleaded, "my wife is about to have a baby, and—"

"Fiancée, Joseph! She's your *fiancée*, not your wife," his relative interjected. "You can sleep out with the animals if you want. But you *cannot* come under my roof."

Extending hospitality to the unwed couple would give approval to their actions, and the whole village would soon find out. Joseph's relative could not risk the shame. So Mary and Joseph remained outside in the courtyard, where the animals were kept at night.

And then it started. Contractions knifed their way through Mary's abdomen, while nervous excitement shivered up Joseph's spine. The piercing pain overshadowed the thick stench of animal excrement that oppressed the cool winter air. And the shame of rejection and ridicule was drowned out by the jubilance of a newborn child.

No doctor, no instruments, no sanitation, and no painkillers. Childbirth in the first century was a risky event. But God endured the shame, the risk, in order to bring us back to Eden.

As Mary grunted and pushed, heaven came crashing down to earth, and Joseph received the Son of God, the snake-crushing Messiah, the illegitimate child, into his arms. First some hair, and then the head. Shoulders and arms, legs and feet. The One who made the stars passed through the birth canal and into Joseph's nervous hands. Joseph slashed and tied the umbilical cord, wiped the blood and birth away from the child's eyes, and assisted his helpless son to expel the remaining fluid from His lungs. Cradling this eight-pound miracle, he watched the breath of life expand the baby's chest, and an urgent wail pierced the courtyard and spooked the sheep. After nursing the child to soothe His fear, Mary wrapped her son—God's Son—in cloth, and with no crib nearby, she laid Him in a feeding trough.

A feeding trough.

The One who spoke the universe into existence, who reigns over the nations, who commands history, who created you and me in His own image chose to be laid in a box where animals ate grain. The One who formed galaxies and molded the earth suckled the breast of a thirteen-year-old unwed Jewish girl in a small village of a backwater province of the Roman Empire.

Jesus is a religious leader, but the religious leaders didn't want Him.

Jesus is a king, but the kings didn't want Him.

Jesus is a revolutionary, but the revolutionaries didn't want Him.

Jesus is the perfect human, but humanity didn't want Him.

You didn't want Him, but He wanted you.

We are hunted and loved by an Ezekiel 16, tent-dwelling God with a beautiful tattoo. And His hunt landed Him in a feeding trough.

JOYFUL PAIN

Jesus was born King of the Jews and King of creation. But the ones who recognized this were pagan astrologers from Babylon and unsettled demons.[3] The undisputed king of the Mediterranean world was in Rome. His name was Caesar Augustus, and his birth was hailed as "good news," or gospel, for the entire world.

When Jesus was born, Augustus had ushered in a time of unprecedented peace and prosperity that made the Reagan years look like the Great Depression. Roads were built, the military was invincible, thieves stayed in their caves, luxury was all around, and distant nations that would otherwise pose a threat kept to themselves. This was the *Pax Romana*—the "peace of Rome"—and Jesus was born right smack-dab in the middle of it.

When Jesus was five years old, Augustus celebrated his twenty-fifth year as the emperor, which happened to be the 750th anniversary of Rome's foundation. Augustus had risen to godlike status, and the people eagerly let him know it. They called Augustus their savior, lord, king of kings, prince of peace, son of God, and the *Pontifex Maximus*, or high priest of Rome, who brought gospels and glad tidings to the people of Rome.

Augustus was a tough act to follow.

So when Jesus's followers also hailed Him as Savior, Lord, King of Kings, Prince of Peace, Son of God, and the *Kohen Gadol*, or High Priest of Israel, who brought the gospel and glad tidings to the entire world, Roman folks certainly raised an eyebrow and, if need be, a sword. The very identity of Jesus challenged the various rulers of the day on every level.

Meanwhile back at the farm, or among the animals, wailed a baby born out of wedlock to a teenage girl in a small village in Judea—a paltry region nestled between the Mediterranean Sea and the desert sands. No pomp or prestige, parades or accolades. The Son of God entered human history in a whisper. Shame, scandal, and humility clothed the birth of Christ, and this is exactly the way He planned it.

God has been pursuing us ever since Eden, and He will stop at nothing. Even if it means laying aside His glory to become one of us. If that's what it takes to *know* us—to attain that authentic, vibrant relationship He longs for—then that's what He will do. God never wanted to relate with us from a distance. He didn't want a cosmic Facebook relationship with His image bearers. He didn't want to tweet us once in a while or shoot us a text to see how we're doing. "Don't have time to call, but just wanted to make sure you're okay." Our God carves our names into His hands. He enters into our pain and finds us under the bridge.

Bethlehem's feeding trough refracts a kaleidoscope of grace, reflected in various passages in the New Testament.

KING OF KINGS, LORD OF LOSERS

Consider Jesus's genealogy in Matthew 1:1–17. In the ancient world, genealogies determined a person's status—whether you came from an honorable family or a shameful one. A person's family line says something about that person. Their character, their social status, the types of people they would hang out with. And Jesus's genealogy says one thing loud and clear: Jesus is right at home with sinners, thugs, and outcasts.

Most genealogies list only the male descendants. Remember, the ancient world was patriarchal. Men were more valued than women, so there was no need to list women—thanks for bearing our children, but we'll take it from here. But Jesus's genealogy lists five women, most of whom have some shady event attached to their name, all of whom we've already met.

The first woman is Tamar, the Canaanite woman who dressed up as a prostitute in order to have sex with her father-in-law, Judah. Her plan succeeded, and she became pregnant with Perez, the one whom God would weave into Jesus's family line.

Next is Rahab, Jericho's down-and-out prostitute, who was the first Canaanite to receive God's grace. Among all the Canaanite leaders, among all the skilled warriors, Rahab was the only one who savored the majesty of Israel's God.

Then there's Ruth, the foreign widow burdening a famished society. A social outcast, a perceived stigma of God's judgment, Ruth was grafted into the messianic line.

Then there's "the wife of Uriah," Bathsheba, who was entangled in the sinful affair with King David—the man who murdered her husband.

Finally, there's Mary, the teenage girl who got pregnant out of wedlock. Though she would become an icon in church tradition, her name was synonymous with shame and scandal in the beginning of the first century.

You thought your family was messed up.

All of these women were social outcasts. They belonged under a bridge. Whether it was their gender, ethnicity, or some sort of sexual debacle, they were rejected by society yet were part of Jesus's genealogy—a tapestry of grace. Not only was God born in a feeding trough to enter our pain, but He chose to be born into a family tree filled with lust, perversion, murder, and deceit. This tells us a lot about the types of people Jesus wants to hang out with. It tells us that Jesus loves Tamars, Judahs, Gomers, and you.

JESUS TABERNACLED

Jesus's manger reveals God's tent-dwelling passion to have an authentic relationship with us. John 1:14 says that "the Word became flesh and [tabernacled] among us, and we have seen his glory, glory as of the only Son from the Father, full of grace and truth." The verb *tabernacled* (usually translated "dwelt") has a rich story behind it, which you already know. It's a story about a God who walked in Eden, dwelled in a tent, and took up residence in the uterus of a teenage girl in order to live among us. When Mary birthed the child and placed Him next to the animals, heaven shook with furious excitement and we were brought one step closer to Eden.

God has a relentless desire not just to save us, forgive us, redeem us, and deliver us from evil but to enjoy us—face-to-face, toe-to-toe, breath to breath, pain upon pain.

Through the manger, God entered into our weakness. Hebrews 4:15 says that Jesus was born "to sympathize with our weaknesses" and describes Him as the One "who in every respect has been tempted as we are, yet without sin." Jesus, in other words, is a man. A real, genuine, blood-filled man. Sometimes our belief in Jesus's deity clouds our understanding of His humanity. But Jesus is a mathematical conundrum—100 percent God *and* 100 percent man. Fully God *and fully human*: a grade A, heart-pumping, excited, sad, energetic, tired, athletic or pudgy, coordinated or clumsy (being cumbersome is not a sin) human. Jesus was not "God in a bod" or some spirit who appeared to be human. He *was* and *is* human.

Jesus was a real human who felt the dull ache of weakness and never sinned. And He experienced the same limitations we possess as humans. Hebrews tells us:

> In the days of his flesh, Jesus offered up prayers and supplications, with loud cries and tears, to him who was able to save him from death, and he was heard because of his reverence. Although he was a son, he learned obedience through what he suffered. (5:7–8)

Jesus didn't just float through life, scoffing at temptation as though it were spoiled milk. His obedience was an agonizing trial that He learned through prayer, perseverance, and many tears (sound familiar?). Jesus was human. The incarnation colors our black-and-white view of grace. The incarnation takes Edenic intimacy to new Himalayan heights.

HUMAN JOY, HUMAN PAIN

God is in control, and He makes up the rules. He could have ordained whatever means He wanted to save us from our sin. If He wanted to, He could have waved His cosmic arm over the earth and forgiven all our sins. He could have snapped His fingers, clapped His hands, or simply spoken a word and we would have been forgiven. He's God and He can do whatever He wants.

But our Edenic tent–God doesn't just want to save us. He actually wants to be with us. He doesn't just love us. God actually likes us. So God removes His royal robes and steps down from His throne to experience—for the first time—what it is like to be human. God is *omniscient*, which means that He is all-knowing. There's nothing in the universe, no piece of information, no fact, no statistic that He doesn't know. The hairs on your head, the zits on your face—He knows about every one. But until the incarnation, God hadn't *experienced* human nature. Since zits aren't a sin, perhaps Jesus had them too.

God knows every hair on your head, but through the incarnation, God knows what it feels like to have hair ripped out.

God knows about tiredness, but through the incarnation, He experiences exhaustion.

God knows how many molecules it takes to shoot a hunger pain from your stomach to your brain. But through the incarnation, God knows what it feels like to starve to the point of death.

Through the incarnation, God has enjoyed the same warm wave of sunlight that splashes across your face on the first day of spring. When you bathe in it, God smiles because He's bathed in it too. He's been refreshed by a night's sleep after a long day of work. Warmed by a toasty bed on a cold winter night. Enjoyed a rich glass of wine while celebrating among friends.

God authored creation. But through the incarnation, God experienced creation. And He encountered joy under the bridge.

He also experienced pain. Relational, psychological, emotional, and physical agony. God has suffered the misery and brokenness of the same sin-saturated world that oppresses us every day. The pain of being rejected, beaten, abused, unloved, uncared for, mocked, shamed, spat upon, and disrespected as an image bearer of the Creator. Jesus knows all of this. He's *experienced* all of this. And He willingly endured it to bring you back to Eden.

The incarnation is a powerful demonstration of grace, since it shows that God doesn't just care for our needs but loves us to the point of *experiencing our needs*. He not only knows our pain, but He has felt our pain. He not only knows when we feel lonely, discouraged, scared, or exhausted—He has been there. "For you know the grace of our Lord Jesus Christ, that though he was rich, yet for your sake he became poor, so that you by his poverty might become rich" (2 Cor. 8:9).

The incarnation is not just a warm-up to the cross and resurrection; it's an essential part of the drama. It's part of God's tattoo. God, out of His own free choice (grace), took the initiative (grace) to step down into our humanity (grace)—and not just any part of humanity, but one clothed with humility and shame (grace)—in order to bridge the gap between God and man (grace) and therefore reclaim that genuine relationship He desires with us (grace).

Gladly burdened to reunite with humanity, God descended into a feeding trough.

9

THUG

This painting is one of my favorites. It's a modern-day rendition of the Last Supper by Scottish artist Peter Howson, and it always provokes a shocking response when I show it to an audience. People are usually offended that the disciples look like scoundrels: leathery faces, gruesome expressions—like something off the cover of an old Iron Maiden album. One of them is wearing a wifebeater and another is smoking a cigar. Surely this could not be the twelve apostles Jesus broke bread with.

Or could it?

When we read the New Testament from a distance, it's tempting to spackle over the offensive stuff with religious familiarity. It's easy to assume, for instance, that the twelve apostles were men who had it all together, or to think that once they met Jesus, all their thuggish tendencies vanished into thin air. But if you brush aside your presuppositions and read the New Testament in its first-century context, you'll see that Howson's painting is much more accurate than the typical stained-glass portraits of the apostles. When Jesus wanted to turn the world upside down, He fought through a crowd of religious leaders and placed His bid on Gomer. Jesus planted the first church on earth with a group of hoodlums who wouldn't be let inside the doors of most churches today. Maybe they would have met under a bridge.

THE TWELVE THUGS

The choosing of the Twelve is one of my favorite stories because grace is sort of tucked underneath the account. It's not really on the surface of the text. The word *grace* doesn't occur in any of the passages about Jesus choosing the Twelve. Nor do we see words like *mercy, love,* or even *forgiveness*. The Bible gives a rather straightforward description of the Twelve, but grace—as we will see—forms the rich soil in which this passage is rooted.

> In these days he went out to the mountain to pray, and all night he continued in prayer to God. And when day came, he called his disciples and chose from them twelve, whom he named apostles: Simon, whom he named Peter, and Andrew his brother, and James and John, and Philip, and Bartholomew, and Matthew, and Thomas, and James the son of Alphaeus, and Simon who was called the Zealot, and Judas the son of James, and Judas Iscariot, who became a traitor. (Luke 6:12–16)

We're not given any insight into the character of these men, nor are there any references to God's grace in their lives. But if you do a character study, you'll see that Jesus handpicked these thugs, not because they were morally upright, but because they weren't. They didn't bring anything to the table. That's precisely why Jesus chose them.

BULL IN A CHINA SHOP

Peter's abrasive character is well-known. When Jesus stoops down to wash Peter's feet, he immediately resists. "Don't wash my feet!" Peter objects. So Jesus clarifies, "If I don't, then you have no part with Me." To which Peter bellows out, "Not just my feet, but my whole body!" Give me a sponge bath, Jesus![1]

A few hours later, when Jesus is praying in the garden the night He is betrayed, He tells His disciples to keep watch, and Peter keeps falling asleep.[2] I can't help but wonder if the three or four glasses of wine Peter had at the Passover meal add weight to his heavy eyes. I don't know.

Peter is always putting his foot in his mouth. When Jesus first tells His disciples that He is going to be crucified, Peter scolds Him. "Far be it from you, Lord! This shall never happen to you" (Matt. 16:22). Jesus replies with His own scathing rebuke: "Get behind me, *Satan*! You are a hindrance to me" (v. 23). What's worse: smoking a cigar or having Jesus call you Satan? Peter—like all of us—has a long way to go in his spiritual journey.

Impatient, impulsive, zealous, a bit slow in the head and quick with his tongue. I love Peter.

One incident that gives me tons of confidence as a Christian is when Peter denies Jesus three times. Peter has been hanging out with Jesus, being mentored by the Creator of the universe. Then someone asks him if he has been with Jesus, and Peter *denies that he even knows Him.*

"Hey, weren't you hanging out with this man from Nazareth?"

"No, sir, I wasn't. I don't even know the man."

Can you imagine if you said this about your wife?

"Are you married to Christine?"

"Christine? Who's Christine? I've never heard of the woman."

Now, I get how scary this could be—Jesus is being hauled off by the authorities and a big, burly soldier with a club asks if you are part of His clan. But according to Matthew, the people who question Peter aren't much of a threat. They aren't soldiers or government authorities, police officers or jailers. The people who ask Peter if he was with Jesus are two slave girls and some random people looking on (Matt. 26:69–75). None of them are carrying clubs.

But Peter's denial of Jesus isn't the end of their relationship. It's only the beginning. Because Peter's commitment to Jesus isn't sustained by Peter. Peter remains committed to Jesus because Jesus is steadily committed to Peter. Just before Peter denies his Lord, Jesus promises to never let him go: "I have prayed for you that your faith may not fail" (Luke 22:32). If it weren't for grace, Peter would be finished.

The same is true for you. Your Bible-reading plan, prayer life, and baptized New Year's resolutions are not what tether God's heart to you. It's because of Jesus—and it will *always, forever be because of Jesus*—that God loves you. If it weren't for grace, we'd all be done for, because there's a little bit of Peter in every one of us. We are all prone to wander. Not only does Jesus not abandon Peter, but He uses him as a major catalyst in establishing His kingdom on earth. Jesus doesn't just put up with Peter—He delights in Peter despite his offensive behavior and never, ever stops pursuing Peter with His grace.

ANGER MANAGEMENT

James and John, the two sons of Zebedee, fascinate me. When I think of these brothers, I usually read them through the lens of their later accomplishments. John goes on to be a well-respected leader and prolific author who writes many books about love. James becomes a leader in Jerusalem's megachurch before being executed for his faith. Surely these two must have been saints.

But actually, they were thugs.

They grew up learning their father's trade as fishermen in a culture where finding work was tough and being successful was even tougher. To make it, you had to have thick skin, stubborn perseverance, and a bit of grit between your teeth. I think James is the one with the stogie in his mouth.

According to Mark 1, Zebedee's fishing business did quite well. We know this because Mark tells us that Zebedee was successful enough to afford "hired servants" (Mark 1:20). Zebedee and his sons grinded out laborious days dragging nets through water. James and John must have developed a lot of tenacity, along with nerves of steel and leathery skin from working long hours on the shadeless shores under the Galilean sun. To run a successful fishing business, you had to be mentally and physically impenetrable.

So when Jesus nicknames them "Sons of Thunder" (Mark 3:17), there's no doubt that everyone knew why. The phrase aptly describes the seething unrest buried in their bones, the shortness of their fuse, their propensity to fly off the handle and clean someone's clock for looking at them wrongly or bumping into their boat. You wouldn't want to mess with these two sons of Zebedee.

And we see this in the Gospels. On one occasion, Jesus and His disciples pass through Samaria—a land hated by the Jews—and one village doesn't let them stay the night. The rest of the disciples are willing to let it slide, but not James and John. They are ready to rumble and loaded for bear. "Lord, do you want us to tell fire to come down from heaven and consume them?" (Luke 9:54).

We often read this statement casually—"Pardon me, sir, but would You fancy us to ask our hallowed Father if He might be interested in warming this village a bit?" But I think we should hear James and John with a New Jersey accent. These two loose cannons would make better bouncers outside an expensive Las Vegas casino owned by a mobster named Lou than followers of Jesus. They get denied from a motel, and they want to nuke the entire village—women and children included.

And think about their pride. They are standing with Jesus, God incarnate, and they want to know if Jesus needs a little help—"Do You want *us* to tell fire to come down from heaven?"

"Jesus, it was pretty cute when You cleansed the lepers, and the whole casting out demons stunt was interesting. But come on, Jesus, we're going to have to call out the big guns for this job."

James and John are two hotheaded thugs whom Jesus uses to plant the first church. Their applications would be stamped "denied" by most of our seminaries.

SUICIDE BOMBER

And then there's Simon the Zealot. We're not sure exactly why he was called "the Zealot." What we do know is that the word *zeal* in its Jewish context does not refer to hyperspiritual pacifists. Quite the opposite. Religious zealots in the Jewish world were violent revolutionaries. In Jesus's day, in fact, there was an official sect of Jews known as the Zealots. They were feisty brawlers with razor-sharp daggers strapped to their thighs. They made it their mission to rid the land of all opposition, even if it meant using violence. Many Jews had such zeal for God and would be ready to fight if need be. But at the top of this list were the Zealots, whose primary identity was their violent aggression toward Rome, Jewish apostates, or anyone who threatened their faith.

There's a good chance that Simon the Zealot was part of this organized religious militia. As such, he would have been a scrapper.

And yes, I think James and John would have gotten along quite well with Simon.

Simon—suicide bomber purchased by Gomer's God.

The one who spent his life killing his enemies would end up loving them; the one who sought to slaughter his persecutors would end up praying for them. The one who was filled with hatred and vengeance would receive and dish out mercy and forgiveness. Such is the power of grace.

TRAITOR, THIEF, THUG

And then there's Levi, whom we know as Matthew—the author of the first gospel. Of all the thugs Jesus handpicked to build His kingdom, I think Matthew was the worst. Luke 5 says that he was a tax collector. Now, you have probably heard that tax collectors were despised by the Jews, but it's hard for us to fathom the depth of their crime. Ancient tax collectors bore a far darker stigma than IRS agents.

In the first century, Rome ruled over Israel. This would be equivalent to, say, Iran, North Korea, or China fighting against, conquering, and then continuing to rule over and oppress America. So imagine that you work hard all day and barely make enough to live on. Still, much of your money goes to fund Iran's development of nuclear weapons so it can continue to rule over and oppress you. Your taxes go to help build beautiful mosques around your town, paper walls with pictures of Iranian leaders, and pay the salary of the abusive soldier who just slapped your wife and kicked your kids because, well, he simply felt like it.

And Matthew—the kid you grew up with, used to play ball with—has betrayed America by working for Iran. They hired him out to be the one who would collect your money.

But he's not working just for them. He's the one who is physically taking your money. Not only is your former friend and patriot helping to fund those oppressing you, but he's also skimming off the top of your paycheck to line his own pockets. You see him daily in the local restaurant, laughing with his new friends, eating expensive steaks, and tossing back exotic drinks as you watch your kids spend night after night doubled over with hunger pains and shame. And bruises from the back of Matthew's hand.

Matthew is the visible extension of everything you hate, and everything that hates you.

In the first century, there were actually two different types of tax collectors, and we see both types in the New Testament. First, there were chief tax collectors like Zacchaeus, that wee little man. Zacchaeus was the boss, a leader of other on-the-ground tax collectors. He was probably higher up on the ladder of social immorality and greed, but as a leader, he probably didn't have to deal with people face-to-face. Then there were regular tax collectors like Matthew, who answered to chief tax collectors like Zacchaeus. Unlike Zacchaeus, Matthew would deal with other Jews face-to-face. He would live within arm's length of those he was oppressing, the very people he grew up with—the very people who wanted him dead.

It's one thing to commit treason, but to commit treason and then continue to swim in the society of the people you have betrayed takes a lot of guts—and indifference.

So Matthew, we can rightly imagine, would have had incredibly thick skin to endure all the insults, threats, dirty looks, and curses. I'm pretty confident the Zealots had a few things to say to Matthew when he took their money. As a man hired to stand on the front lines, I'm sure Matthew could hold his own in a fight. Matthew would have to wrench money from Jewish hands, and any sort of stubborn resistance would be quickly beaten down by Matthew's violent fists. I think Matthew's the thug wearing the wifebeater.

On a moral level, tax collectors were not just people who did bad things. Many of them actively engaged in perverted and morally disgusting lifestyles in the eyes of the people. Tax collectors of the first century, like Zacchaeus and Matthew, would have rivaled the pimps, porn stars, and pedophiles of our world. According to Jewish tradition, they were considered equivalent to thieves and murderers and socially worse than dung collectors. Religious Jews considered tax collectors to be beyond the point of repentance. Grace's leash stopped well out of reach of the tax collectors. They were just too bad to receive God's stubborn delight.

FRAT PARTY

I can't help but think about the crowd that Matthew invites to celebrate his conversion. Luke tells us that right after Matthew gets saved, he throws a huge party to celebrate with all his friends. Since none of them are religious—or even moral—this must be quite the scene, which Luke describes as a "large company of tax collectors and others" (Luke 5:29–30) lying around the room, boozing it up. A first-century frat party.

In modern terms, this crowd is the dregs of society, the bottom of the barrel, a room filled with gangsters, hookers, and drug dealers. If such a crowd invited you to a party, would you go? Jesus would. He went to Matthew's. After all, "those who are well have no need of a physician, but those who are sick" (Luke 5:31). Jesus wasn't born in a feeding trough so He could don a sport jacket and go to church in the suburbs. He sucked in the stench of the manger so He could sniff out some thugs to help Him build a kingdom.

Matthew was an immoral Jewish apostate who committed political and religious treason. I can't help but wonder how Simon the *Zealot* and Matthew the *tax collector* got along. This would be like starting a church with a leader of the KKK and a member of the Black Panther movement. I'm pretty sure both Simon and Matthew had one eye open at their first prayer meeting.

There's one other thug Jesus invited into His kingdom-building entourage who deserves mention. This thug is not one of the Twelve, though some consider her an apostle. Her name is Mary Magdalene, and Jesus's kingdom would not have been the same without her.

CREEPY BAG LADY

Mary Magdalene is one of the most well-known and yet misconstrued women in the Bible. She's often portrayed in Christian art as a forgiven prostitute, but nowhere in the New Testament is she depicted as such.[3] Dan Brown's description of Mary as Jesus's wife in *The Da Vinci Code* is even further from the truth. Neither of these views has a shred of biblical evidence to support it.

The only description we have of Mary is in Luke 8:2, where it says that Jesus cast out seven demons from her. The number seven is interesting. It may be literal—she had exactly seven demons that terrorized her. But the number seven often means completeness and isn't to be taken literally, and this is probably the intention here. Mary Magdalene was totally controlled by demons when she met Jesus.

Being overrun by demons, Mary probably looked insane. The villagers would have looked at her with horror, disdain, and disgust. She probably had no friends, certainly no husband or any man who would take the slightest interest in her. Society rejected her. It was repulsed by her. She probably had to beg for money—if anyone was willing to come close enough to drop a shekel in her cup. Mary Magdalene was the epitome of social rejection.

A toothless bag lady who walks down the street muttering and arguing with herself. If you look at her, she cusses at you; keep looking, and she'll throw a rock. That's Mary Magdalene.

Put yourself in Mary's shoes.

Imagine everyone who knows you thinks you're a nuisance, you smell horrible, and you have nothing to offer. Imagine that this is your life—and has been for as long as you can remember. Your mother and father have abandoned you. Your brothers and sisters have disowned you. You've heard the word *friendship*, but you've never known what it means. You've seen people laugh, but you've never experienced the sensation. Every now and then strangers approach you, but just when you think they're going to talk to you, they kick dust in your direction, spit on you, and then walk away.

And then, a young Jewish rabbi walks up, surrounded by a bunch of men—and you think you're done for. *How many wads of phlegm will cover my face before they kick me, beat me, and gang-rape me. Is this my death?*

But instead of death, the rabbi offers a tender hand, gently raises you up from the ground, and commands the demons to leave you. "This woman is *Mine*! I value her. I delight in her. And you have no business here anymore—Mary is My disciple. And I need her to build My kingdom. *Be gone!*"

Mary breathes for the first time the breath of life.

She now knows what friendship means. She feels a strange sensation welling up and tickling her throat. It's called laughter. And now, for the first time, she knows what it means to be human.

More than all the other disciples, Mary Magdalene remains singularly committed to Jesus. None of the male disciples of Jesus are as unshakably sold out for Jesus as Mary Magdalene. We see this at Jesus's crucifixion, burial, and resurrection. At the end of Jesus's life, when the Jewish leaders and Roman rulers turn up the heat on Jesus, and His disciples see that things are taking a turn for the worse, many of Jesus's disciples scatter. Judas betrays Him. Peter denies Him. And the other disciples are nowhere to be found.

But Mary. Mary Magdalene. She can't leave Jesus. Where would she go? Who else can fill her lungs with the fresh air of Eden?

And so in the gospel accounts of Matthew, Mark, and Luke, it's Mary Magdalene who stands firm beneath the cross and beside the tomb, and it's Mary who races to the grave that Sunday morning to be with her Savior and Friend, only to find Him risen from the dead. When Jesus breaks the chains of death and conquers the power of

Satan, it is Mary who first basks in the glory of the risen King—all
because the Creator has set His undeserved affection on a woman in
the gutter.

CHARIS—THE STUFF THUGS ARE MADE OF

I think many Christians are willing to put up with social outcasts and
misfits, but this isn't grace. It's tolerance. Where there's no pursuit,
no stubborn delight, there's a superficial Christianese grace ("bless
this food to our bodies"), but it's not *charis*. God aggressively and
delightfully *values* and *uses* thugs and misfits to build His glorious kingdom: abrasive, thickheaded people like Peter, hotheaded
racists like James and John, violent brawlers and extortionists like
Simon and Matthew, and mentally deranged bag ladies like Mary
Magdalene. He doesn't give them a bowl of soup and shuffle them
out of the church. He gives them responsibility—the hallmark of
genuine value—and trusts in the God who uses the weak to shame
the strong.

Grace isn't a term. It's not a doctrine. It's not a buzzword. It's not
the words of a song, a prayer before meals, a name plastered on our
churches. It's not leniency or niceness. It's not something that can be
domesticated or completely understood. And it's something that can
never grow old or stale.

Grace is what flows through the veins of Jesus, whose heart stubbornly beats for you—a thug loved by the One who gladly endured
the cross to bring you back to Eden.

10

IT IS FINISHED

AMISH GRACE

On October 2, 2006, Charles Roberts entered a one-room school-house in a Pennsylvanian Amish community. Armed with a 9mm handgun, a 12-gauge shotgun, and a .30-06 rifle, Roberts told the male children to leave the room before he barricaded himself inside. He then instructed the ten remaining girls between the age of six and twelve to line up facing the back wall of the classroom. Filled with anger over the tragic loss of his own daughter, Roberts vented his wrath on ten innocent Amish girls. Roberts sprayed the room with bullets, and several pierced the skulls of five girls. Immediately, they crumpled to their deaths. Others were critically injured. Roberts then shoved the gun into his mouth and sent one final bullet sailing through his brain. Charles Roberts fell dead.

I'll never forget being hammered by that story when it first went public. I was stunned beyond words. Why would a man kill a bunch of Amish girls, the epitome of innocence? I had two daughters of my own at the time and one more on the way. Now, eight years later, my three daughters are all within the ages of the schoolgirls who were slaughtered that day in Pennsylvania. I find it hard to tame the fury that burns in my heart when I imagine my daughters being gunned down by a sadistic killer.

The only thing more difficult to tame was the grace that the Amish poured out liberally on the one who *did* gun down their daughters.

While my mind fixates on justice, the friends and fathers of the murdered girls pursued forgiveness. "We must not think evil of this man," one grandfather instructed the community. Another Amish father reminded them that Roberts "had a mother and a wife and a soul and now he's standing before a just God." A few hours after the shooting, several from the Amish community visited the wife of the killer to comfort her, offering reassurance that they had forgiven her husband for firing bullets through their daughters' heads. Another Amish man held the killer's father in his arms for over an hour. In the aftermath, the Amish community set up a charitable gift fund to help alleviate the financial stress of Roberts's widow—a small token of unconditional love.[1]

When Roberts deserved justice, the Amish offered love.

The killing that day shocked the world. But it was the Amish response of unconditional forgiveness that created a wave of variegated reactions. Some were impressed by such forgiveness. Others were critical, saying child killers should be hated, not forgiven. As for Marie Roberts, the wife of the killer, their forgiveness changed her heart, and, in her own words, it changed the *world*. She wrote an open letter to her Amish neighbors thanking them for their forgiveness, saying:

> Your love for our family has helped to provide the healing we so desperately need. Gifts you've given

have touched our hearts in a way no words can describe. Your compassion has reached beyond our family, beyond our community, and *is changing our world.*[2]

Marie is onto something here. Performing random acts of kindness doesn't change the world. Doing nice things for nice people doesn't change the world. Returning a wallet to the one who left it at the restaurant is a kind gesture, but it won't change the world.

Jesus wants to change the world.

Only unconditional, stubborn love toward your enemy produces ripple effects strong enough to change the world.

The Amish forgiveness mirrors Christ's forgiving love that spilled from His veins on Calvary. If the Amish response feels counterintuitive, if Jesus's cross has lost its offense as it dangles around your neck, then you need to revisit the cross.

If you aren't challenged by the scandal of God dying for His enemies; if you aren't stunned by Jesus beckoning the prostitutes to embrace their free pardon; if you haven't wept at Jesus's joyful pain on the splintery beam; if you aren't outraged by an unrobed King of Kings and Lord of Lords turning the other check, resisting retaliation, loving those on death row—we were all on death row—against all human logic, against all cultural norms, against every innate sense of justice; and if your stubborn inability to love your own enemy has not driven you back again and again to Calvary and the vacant tomb, where it was declared "it is finished, it is finished, it is finished," then I would suggest that you have not meditated on the scandal of the cross long enough. The message of God crucified should never get old. And grace—*charis*—should never be neutered and chained up inside the gated community.

ENEMY LOVE

Paul put it like this:

> For one will scarcely die for a righteous person—though perhaps for a good person one would dare even to die—but God shows his love for us in that while we were still sinners, Christ died for us.… For if while we were enemies we were reconciled to God by the death of his Son, much more, now that we are reconciled, shall we be saved by his life. (Rom. 5:7–8, 10)

No one likes to be considered an enemy. But that's what the Bible calls us. We are enemies, loved and pursued by our Creator, who will stop at nothing to reconcile us to Himself. Such reconciliation happened on the cross—the grand finale (yes, there'll be an encore) of the narrative of grace we have been following. Unlike the final episode of *Lost*, Calvary brings it all together and makes sense of the whole story.

The transcendent and intimate God of Genesis 1 and 2 is the same God who walks alone and handpicks Perez to carry the promise; the same God who cares for Rahab, provides for Ruth, and values all the undervalued women who help the sea part in two; yes, the God who camps in a tent for hundreds of years, who uses a tongue-tied murderer and a music-writing murderer and a Philistine-loving murderer to build a kingdom. He's the same God who rescues Ezekiel's abandoned child and purchases Hosea's whore—the same God who hangs on a tree with a spike driven right through each of His tattooed hands.

NAIL, CROWN, AND GLORY

We have castrated the symbol of the cross. Celebrities would never wear an electric chair around their neck, but that's what the cross was—a gruesome punishment for capital crimes. In fact, crucifixion was the result of many years of cruel ingenuity. Barbaric cultures teamed together to invent the most painful, shameful, and unspeakable way to torture a criminal, which at the same time deterred future criminals from making the same mistake. Crucifixion was first invented by the Persians, who used to impale victims of a conquered city on long, sharp poles shoved in the ground outside the city's walls. Impalement was sometimes replaced with nailing a victim to a nearby tree and leaving him for dead. In time, the two methods were combined, and soldiers would pin their victims to long wooden posts instead of trees.

Other nations refined the torture. Parthians, Greeks, and Phoenicians found crucifixion to be an effective way to brutalize their enemies. But it was Rome that took what the Persians invented and perfected it.

First, Rome added scourging to the mix. Prior to crucifixion, Roman soldiers lashed the victim with leather whips embedded with metal balls or sharp pieces of sheep bone. The lacerations flayed the victim's back until his muscles were pulverized and his ribs were exposed. Sometimes the pain and blood loss were too great, and the criminal died before making it to the cross.

Then, Rome added a horizontal crossbeam to Persia's single pole, giving us the cross-shaped image we know today. Rome had set up many permanent vertical posts around major cities, especially those that were prone to revolt, like Jerusalem. When a criminal was crucified, he would first be forced to carry the horizontal crossbeam, weighing about one hundred pounds, on his shoulders through the streets of the city to the place where the vertical post stood. His wrists were then pinned to the crossbeam with six-inch spikes. Next, the criminal and the crossbeam were hoisted up to the permanent post, secured either by rope or by a mortise-and-tenon joint. Then the victim's feet were nailed to the base of the cross, either through the foot or through the ankle, as one archaeological discovery has revealed.

Back flayed, wrists pierced, muscle and bone exposed, blood steadily draining. Not the sort of scene one should hang as an ornament around the neck. Still, we do.

But this is only the beginning.

Thanks to adrenal glands, the human body can endure more pain than you think. Most often, death came slowly, though each minute on the cross felt like eternity. Since the crucified criminal was hanging from spikes, breathing was tremendously difficult. To gather a breath, he had to push down on his pierced feet, but this could last only so long. So in order to prolong the torture, Rome added a new feature to the cross: a small seat halfway up the cross to give the victim a source of rest and to make breathing easier. Their intention wasn't to dull the pain but to prolong it. Just when the victim couldn't suck in another painful breath, human reflex and the will to survive would force him to sit—to hang on to the thread of life as long as he could. And don't forget, his hamburgered back inched up and down the splintery wood with each agonizing breath. Thirty times a minute, 1,800 times an hour—in the case of Jesus, for six hours.

Crucifixion was so horrific that Roman authors rarely talked about it. Cicero, the Roman statesman and prolific writer, left behind a few scattered statements about the horror, calling it "the most cruel and disgusting penalty."[3] The Jewish historian Josephus called it "the most wretched of deaths."[4] So monstrous was the punishment that Roman citizens were exempt. Instead, the cross was reserved for those on the lower rung of the social ladder: slaves, insurrectionists, and soldiers who committed treason. And when some authorities raised the question whether Roman citizens should not be exempt, the people were appalled. Such barbarism should be reserved only for the dregs of society.

Death came from various causes. Sometimes it was loss of blood. Other times it was suffocation, as the victim lost all strength to take one more breath. In some cases, the criminal was slowly eaten by wild animals in the night. Jesus was spared this form of death. Instead, He probably drowned in the pool of blood that filled His lungs.

Since we live in a culture that is allergic to pain, we often focus on the bodily torment Jesus endured. But the Mediterranean world was an "honor-shame" culture, where public shame was the greatest horror. And this was the primary design of the cross: to shame the victim and his family, friends, and anyone who followed him.[5] This is why criminals were crucified on the highways outside the city gates where all could see. This is why the victim was stripped naked for all to behold. This is why a multilingual sign was secured above the cross, inscribed with the victim's crimes. And this is why most crucified victims, contrary to popular depictions, hung only a few feet above the ground. This way, the populace could nearly come face-to-face with the criminal—a perfect spot to hurl insults and wads of saliva.

Such is the narrative of love.

Jesus could have been beheaded like His cousin John, or He could have been stoned to death. As long as He died as the perfect sacrifice, God's wrath would have been satisfied and forgiveness would have flowed freely. But God wanted to do more than just satisfy His wrath and forgive our sin. He wanted to stretch out His bloody, tattooed hands for all to see. Broadcast across the splintery tree whose roots plunged down deep, reaching the rich soil of Eden.

Hebrews tells us that it was "for the joy that was set before him" that Jesus "endured the cross" (12:2). The joy of being reconciled and reunited with His image-bearing-masterpieces-turned-enemies, who deserve wrath, not forgiveness, justice, not grace. Joy—for you—is what kept Jesus going. Through every slash of the whip, every pound of the nail, every agonizing breath, every shameful insult hurled from the mouths of His beloved enemies—it was for Jesus's stubborn delight set before Him that He endured the cross. The ingenuity of the Persians, the barbaric fine-tuning of the Romans, the wood, spikes, hammers, splinters, and crown of thorns picked from a garden are all woven into the tapestry of grace as the only fitting way to capture God's love for His image bearers.

This is why you can't make God love you. God loves you because of God. God acted in Jesus out of His own freedom to

descend into a feeding trough and spread His arms across a splintery beam of wood.

It was Jesus's declaration "It is finished" that made God love
you.[6]

IT IS FINISHED

And when Jesus declared, "It is finished," He meant it. God's punishment for our sin was paid for, permanently settled, finished—100
percent. If you have responded in faith to God's free pardon through
Jesus, then God will never punish you for your sin. It's finished.
No more. If you screw up today or tomorrow (which you will), it's
already been paid for through Jesus. "There is therefore now no condemnation for those who are in Christ Jesus," Paul said (Rom. 8:1).
None. God will not and cannot condemn you after He has already
condemned Jesus for you. It's impossible. God will never be angry
with you since His anger was poured out on Jesus. All of it. One
hundred percent.

This point needs to soak into your bones, because we have a
natural desire to cover our shame with guilt instead of grace. Guilt
drags along behind us like a ball and chain, even though God has
shattered the chain with a cross. A friend I'll call Natalie carried such
guilt around for years. When she was a teenager, her boyfriend broke
up with her because they were fooling around too much and he felt
guilty. The message was loud and clear: Natalie was the source of sin
in his otherwise solid walk with Christ.

Years later, she was in a bridal shop, looking for a wedding dress.
But her guilt followed her through the door. At the sight of herself in

one of those dresses, she panicked and fled the shop in tears. White is a symbol of purity, and she had failed.

But grace tells us that such purity is blood bought. Purity rings can't make us truly pure, even if we keep our commitment. Only Jesus can make us pure, and even though she was part of a less-than-perfect relationship as a teenager, she was pure, in the eyes of Christ, through His cross.

When Jesus said, "It is finished," He meant it. His blood doesn't cover 90 percent of our sin, but all of it. Past, present, and future. It even covers impure teenage relationships. No, you didn't earn that white dress. But Jesus did.

I have also spoken to many people who believe that the bad things that happen to them are God's punishment for their sins. An illness, failure to find a mate, even the death of a child—it must be God's judgment. But the gospel cannot be understood in terms of such tit-for-tat retribution—do this and get blessed; don't do this and get cursed. The gospel blows apart the categories of transaction and conditionality, as Tullian Tchividjian (my favorite preacher of grace) has eloquently stated:

> Like Job's three friends, we naturally conclude that good people get good stuff and bad people get bad stuff. The idea that bad people get good stuff is thickly counterintuitive; it seems terribly unfair and offends our sense of justice. Even those of us who have tasted the radical saving grace of God find it intuitively difficult *not* to put conditions on grace.... Grace is radically unbalanced. It has no

"but"; it is unconditional, uncontrollable, unpre-
dictable, and undomesticated.[7]

We're hardwired to believe that good people get the good stuff
and bad people get the bad stuff, as Tullian says. But the gospel
demands that bad people get the good stuff, and we're all bad! Or
again, God justifies His enemies (Rom. 4:4–5) and gives Himself to
the godless (Rom. 5:8–11). Any attempt to sustain God's love for
you through self-effort—making God love you—will end in failure
and ultimately offend the One who joyfully declared, "It is finished."

We must not sanctify the scandal of God's love for His *enemies*.

REDEMPTION

Chuck Colson tells a story about twenty American soldiers held cap-
tive during World War II. During their captivity, they were forced
to do hard labor, which usually involved digging with a shovel. One
morning, the soldiers showed up for duty one shovel short. The
prison guard counted twenty prisoners but only nineteen shovels,
and he threatened to kill five prisoners if the one who forgot his
shovel didn't fess up. Seconds later, a prisoner stepped forward and
admitted that he forgot his shovel. The guard quickly unbuckled his
pistol, shoved the barrel into the temple of the shovel-less prisoner,
and pulled the trigger. Still furious, the guard threatened the others
with the same fate if they forget their shovels. But after taking a
recount, the guard found twenty shovels after all. The first time
around, the guard simply miscounted. The innocent prisoner gave
his life for his friends and comrades.

This is grace.

Or is it?

The soldier's heroic act reveals a form of grace, but it's not *charis*. The story may have moved your heart (it did mine), but it falls short of biblical grace. The soldier's heroism is an *inferior* analogy to Jesus's love and sacrifice for you. Jesus didn't give His life for His comrades and friends—buddies on the battlefield who earned His trust and were worthy of sacrifice. Jesus died for His enemies.

The psychotic cannibal who had sex with and ate portions of seventeen people.

The pharisaic church kid who memorized God from a distance.

The pagan patriarch who trusted in lies rather than his Lord.

The promiscuous father who impregnated his promiscuous daughter-in-law.

The Canaanite harlot trying to put bread on the table by lying on her back.

The down-and-out immigrant living in a foreign land.

David, Gomer, Mary, and Matthew. Peter, James, John, the misfits living under a bridge. Simon, soccer moms, and that worthless bag lady from Magdala.

Charis—God's stubborn delight in His enemies—has redeemed them all, thundering from heaven to enter our pain. To forgive us. To save us. To enjoy us. To pursue us from prison and bring us to paradise—to dance with our Creator in the splendor of Eden.

EPILOGUE:

. . . .

WHERE DOES OBEDIENCE FIT IN?

HOW MUCH SIN CAN I GET AWAY WITH?

If God loves His enemies, then should I live like an enemy? If Hosea unconditionally loved Gomer, then should I try to live like Gomer? If God used Judah to redeem the world, then can I venture to the nearest street corner and find my own Tamar?

These questions are as old as the apostle Paul, who asked the rhetorical question, "Are we to continue in sin that grace may abound?" (Rom. 6:1).

Admittedly, I've been pushing hard on the truth that God loves people unconditionally; that God pursues His enemies with grace; that there's nothing you can do to make God love you. So how do we answer Paul's question? Should we live like Rahab in order to get more grace from God?

I'm going to agree with Paul on this one: "By no means!" (Rom. 6:2). As Christians, we should vigorously seek to obey God and should try our hardest not to sin. The Christian life is a race, and we should run it with all our might.

This may seem confusing. In all my talk on grace, how could I say that we should vigorously obey? That's because obedience is not grace's enemy. They are friends, partners, related like Siamese twins.

If after reading this book you are eager to know, "How much can I now sin and still be right with God?" then you need to read the book again. There's a good chance you haven't truly understood the God we have been talking about. If hearing about the God of Tamar, Ruth, and Gomer stirs up an eagerness to reject that God and not desire an obedient relationship with Him, then something didn't register. God will chase you, but why run?

ENERGISM

The relationship between grace and obedience is a gnarly issue, and I don't want to bog down the discussion by hacking our way through a theological jungle. In general, there are three different explanations Christians give to how grace relates to obedience.

Some Christians say that obedience is good but not necessary. What Christians do or don't do is icing on the cake. It would be good for you to respond to Jesus with obedience, but either way, we're still saved by grace through faith. If we smuggle obedience in the back door of salvation, then grace is no longer grace. We'll call this the "free grace" view. And mind you: this is *not* what I've been describing in this book.

Others say that God has done His part and that now it's our turn to do our part. God saves, but we are responsible for obedience. God is certainly available to counsel us when we need Him, and He has call-waiting. But ultimately, it's up to us to work out our salvation.

I don't think either of these views accurately captures the relationship between grace and obedience. Because neither of them talks about *energism*.

Energism is the third view, and to my mind, it's the most accurate way to understand the relationship between grace and obedience.

The word *energism* was coined by New Testament scholar John Barclay.[1] He came up with it after studying Galatians 2:8, where Paul said that the same God who "worked [*energesas*] through Peter for his apostolic ministry to the circumcised worked [*energesen*] also through me for mine to the Gentiles." The word *worked* translates the Greek word *energeo*, from which we get the word *energy*. Here, Paul talked about God working in and through Peter and Paul in their ministries. And in the very next verse, Paul described these same ministries in terms of "the grace that was given" to both Peter and himself.

God, in His grace, worked in Peter and Paul—two sinners unworthy of favor and incapable of doing anything on their own—to take the message of Jesus to the ends of the earth.

Energism, therefore, refers to God working in and through us to do His will. If we talk about obedience as our response to God—God does His part; now we do ours—this places too big of a wedge between God's work and ours. When we get saved, we become united with Christ and indwelt by the Spirit, so that it's impossible to untangle Christ's empowering presence, the Spirit's transformative work, and our own regenerated response to God.

That last line was heavy, I know. We'll come back to it shortly. But first, let's keep unpacking *energism*.

GRACE WORKS HARD

Paul talked about *energism* again in 1 Corinthians 15:9–10. Read this passage slowly; it packs a powerful punch:

> For I am the least of the apostles, unworthy to be called an apostle, because I persecuted the church of God. But by the grace of God I am what I am, and his grace toward me was not in vain. On the contrary, I worked harder than any of them, though it was not I, but the grace of God that is with me.

Much like Dahmer, Judah, or the trolls under Waco's bridge, Paul didn't bring any merit to the table when God saved him. Like all of us, Paul was saved by grace. But what was Paul's response? He worked. In fact, he "worked harder than any of them" (probably referring to the other apostles). But look at how Paul integrated grace into the scene. He didn't say that God saved him and then left him the keys to finish the race—thanks, God, I'll take it from here. Neither did he say that obedience was optional. Paul's obedience, rather, was the natural—or *supernatural*—by-product of God's grace. Any ounce of obedience produced by Paul was ultimately the result of grace—"by the grace of God I am what I am." And if there were no obedience, then "his grace toward" Paul would have been "in vain."

Lack of obedience reveals a lack of grace. Divine grace produces the obedience God demands.

WORK OUT YOUR SALVATION

Obedience can't be icing on the cake, because grace doesn't stop pursuing us when we get saved. It continues on to push good works out the other side. Grace is just that powerful. Paul said it like this in Philippians 2:

> Therefore, my beloved, as you have always obeyed,
> so now, not only as in my presence but much more
> in my absence, work out your own salvation with
> fear and trembling, for it is God who works in you,
> both to will and to work for his good pleasure. (vv.
> 12–13)

Be sure to note that Paul said, "Work *out* [not work *for*] your own salvation." In other words, do something in response to what God has done for you. But just to make sure that we don't separate the work of God from our own effort—thinking that we must pick up where God left off—Paul highlighted God's ongoing work of grace in and through us: "For it is God who works [*energon*] in you, both to will and to work for his good pleasure" (v. 13). More than just our obedience, Paul said that the very *desire* to obey comes from God.

Energism. When you do something good, it's because grace is working in you. When you obey, that's grace doing its job. The instant that desire flares up in your soul to do a good deed, that's grace too. Because grace doesn't just park at salvation, get out, and hand you the keys.

This is why I think the "free grace" view discussed earlier falls short of biblical *charis*. It's too weak. Too out of shape. It runs out of gas once we get converted. "Free grace" stumbles off the track once it passes us the baton. Biblical *charis* passes the baton but keeps running alongside us, encouraging us, slipping us gel packs and Gatorade. When we stumble, it picks us up. When we fall to the ground and snap our shin, *charis* throws us on its back and carries us through the finish line. We're running the race and our muscles get sore, but we'll never cross the finish line apart from grace. And once we cross the line, we'll realize that all of that adrenaline running through our veins was grace as well.

Or as Paul said in Galatians:

> I have been crucified with Christ. It is no longer I
> who live, but Christ who lives in me. And the life
> I now live in the flesh I live by faith in the Son of
> God, who loved me and gave himself for me. (2:20)

Jesus and His finished work are not just the motivation for obedience, but its enabler. Jesus's life, death, and resurrection don't just take care of your past sins, giving you a fresh start. Rather, Christ's work is the energy, the fuel, the ongoing power to do the impossible: render joyful obedience to your Creator.

CLOTHED WITH CHRIST

When you get saved, something cosmic happens. Jesus and you become one. Not in a weird Hindu sense, but in such a way that

Jesus's ongoing presence and your ongoing desire to follow Him become inseparable. "The more the human agent is operative, the more (not the less) may be attributed to God," said John Barclay.[2] When we obey, that's evidence of *God's* work in us.

In fact, Paul's favorite description of salvation, one he used more than "justification," "redemption," or "forgiveness" combined, is his short little phrase "in Christ." More than a hundred times, Paul talked about our union with Christ by the phrase "in Christ" or "in Him." When you get saved, you are joined with Christ. No longer can you think of yourself apart from Him, and no longer does He see Himself apart from you. You are grafted into His death, burial, and resurrection; you are part of His body, His temple, His new creation. You have been clothed with Christ, baptized into Christ, resurrected with Christ, and your life is now His and His life is now yours. You have been wedded to the obedient One, the One who lived a perfect life, died a perfect death, and was raised from the dead to sit at the right hand of the Father, where He reigns over the universe.

All of this is summed up in Ephesians 2:

> But God, being rich in mercy, because of the great love with which he loved us, even when we were dead in our trespasses, made us alive together with Christ—by grace you have been saved—and raised us up with him and seated us with him in the heavenly places in Christ Jesus, so that in the coming ages he might show the immeasurable riches of his grace in kindness toward us in Christ Jesus. (vv. 4–7)

We are alive with Christ and raised up with Christ, and our identity will forever be swallowed up in Him. When we obey, it's not so much that we respond to His grace but that we are living out our new identity in Him. By His power, by His Spirit, by His grace. He is living in us, and we are living in Him.

ABIDE AND OBEY

When we are tapped into Jesus and the Spirit, grace flows through our veins and compels us to obey. We should never think of our obedience as separate from God's work in us. Rather, our response to God is the by-product of God's work in us. As Jesus famously said in John 15:

> As the branch cannot bear fruit by itself, unless it abides in the vine, neither can you, unless you abide in me. I am the vine; you are the branches. Whoever abides in me and I in him, he it is that bears much fruit, for apart from me you can do nothing. (vv. 4–5)

When branches are connected to a nutrient-rich vine, they produce grapes. It's inevitable. And when people are connected to Christ through faith, they produce obedience. It, too, is inevitable. This is why Jesus can confidently say, "*If* you love me, you *will* keep my commandments" (John 14:15). He's not encouraging us to grit our teeth, double up our devotions, and muscle our way through the pearly gates. Rather, He tells us to *abide*: to look to the One who enables us to obey. To submit to the Spirit, who gives us the ability to render good works to God.

In saying this, I'm not denying grace, but showcasing it. Again, obedience isn't grace's enemy, but its by-product. Divine grace is so relentless, so powerful, so committed to transform sinners into saints that it will keep chipping away at our sin-encrusted humanity until it finds and releases our Edenic beauty. And when we resist—when we fall back into sin—there's still no condemnation, no wrath, no punishment. There's only grace. There will always be only grace, ready to roll up its sleeves, delightfully meet us in our filth, and pull us out of the sewer again and again. When you sleep with your boyfriend, look at porn, take one too many drinks, or think too highly of yourself, there is grace. Not mere leniency, or unconditional acceptance, as if God couldn't care less about your holiness. When we fall into sin, there is God's stubborn delight and pursuit of fragile people who are running from him. We are all, as Robert Robinson wrote in his well-known hymn "Come, Thou Fount of Every Blessing," "prone to wander … prone to leave the God I love." We are prone to wander, but God is prone to pursue. And He's faster.

THE VINEYARD

So let's revisit that theologically loaded phrase: *When we get saved, we become united with Christ and indwelt by the Spirit, so that it's impossible to untangle Christ's empowering presence, the Spirit's transformative work, and our own regenerated response to God.* Our union with Christ drives us to obey. Our will, emotions, and desires are meshed with His. The Spirit who indwells us empowers us to obey. We have been clothed with the risen Christ, so we cannot understand ourselves apart from Him. With such cosmic artillery, it's impossible that a genuine Christ follower—clothed with the righteousness of Christ, indwelt by the Holy Spirit—will not render obedience to God. We say with Paul, "Not I, but the grace of God that is with me" (1 Cor. 15:10).

This is why I stand by everything I've said in this book and yet can also say that our obedience is vital for our Christian existence.

Our obedience doesn't determine God's love toward us, any more than grapes force the sun to pour out its heat upon the vine. It's the sun's heat (God's love), the rich soil (Jesus's death and resurrection), and the abundant water (the Spirit) that produce grapes.

Or we can switch it around a bit.

The Vinedresser enjoys the vine. He cares for it. Nurtures it. Thinks about it often. He *prunes* it. And apart from the Vinedresser, there would be no grapes. But what about that bad year? There was a drought. A fire. A big rig lost control on the nearby highway and careened into the vineyard. And there's no fruit that year. Maybe a grape here and there, but they're small, shriveled—hardly noticeable. It's been a bad year, and the Vinedresser is working extra hard to make next year's crop more fruitful. Maybe some extra pruning will do the trick.

The Vinedresser is grieved, and He's certainly not thrilled over the shriveled grapes. But He still loves being a Vinedresser, and He's still passionate about His vine.

The number of grapes—some years there are none—doesn't determine, sustain, or elevate the Vinedresser's enjoyment of making wine.

CHARIS

Such is the power and scandal of grace. It challenges and relieves, comforts and convicts, provokes and forgives. If you're glued to your couch, it'll pry you off. If you're dragging a ball of guilt around, it'll snap the chain. Grace—God's stubborn delight in you—snuffs out apathy and brings healing to trolls under the bridge. If you're living in sin, don't run from grace. Run to it. You don't possess the moral power to create obedience. Only God does.

NOTES

FOREWORD

1. Paul Zahl, *Grace in Practice* (Grand Rapids, MI: Eerdmans, 2007), 36.

2. Robert Farrar Capon, *The Romance of the Word: One Man's Love Affair with Theology* (Grand Rapids, MI: Eerdmans, 1996), 10.

3. Robert Farrar Capon, *Between Noon and Three: Romance, Law, and the Outrage of Grace* (New York: Harper & Row, 1982), 7.

CHAPTER 1

1. Ratcliff's encounter with Dahmer is retold in his book, with Lindy Adams, *Dark Journey, Deep Grace: Jeffrey Dahmer's Story of Faith* (Abilene, TX: Leafwood, 2006).

2. I'm pretty sure that Tullian Tchividjian has said something like this in one of his many sermons on grace.

3. C. S. Lewis used a phrase similar to "real ingredient of divine happiness" in *The Weight of Glory* (New York: HarperCollins, 2009), 39.

CHAPTER 2

1. Rick Warren, *The Purpose Driven Life* (Grand Rapids, MI: Zondervan, 2002), 17.

2. Gordon J. Wenham, *Genesis 1–15*, vol. 1 of Word Biblical Commentary (Waco, TX: Word, 1987), 59.

3. Zsa Zsa Palagyi, "A Simple Invitation Leads to New Life," The 700 Club, accessed July 31, 2013, www.cbn.com/700club/features/amazing/ZP96_Cynthia_Shaver.aspx.

4. "Child Sexual Abuse Statistics," National Center for Victims of Crime, victimsofcrime.org, accessed July 31, 2013, www.victimsofcrime.org/media/reporting-on-child-sexual-abuse/child-sexual-abuse-statistics.

5. Jenifer Goodwin, "Rate of Eating Disorders in Kids Keeps Rising," *U.S. News & World Report*, November 29, 2010, http://health.usnews.com/health-news/family-health/brain-and-behavior/articles/2010/11/29/rate-of-eating-disorders-in-kids-keeps-rising.

CHAPTER 3

1. Whatever "knowledge of good and evil" means, the point is that they assert their own autonomy, making up their own rules and living by them.

2. Rom. 8:19–23.

3. See, for instance, the Epic of Atrahasis and the *Enuma Elish*.

4. For Ur in Abraham's time, see Alfred J. Hoerth, *Archaeology and the Old Testament* (Grand Rapids, MI: Baker, 1998), 59–71.

5. For the Jewish tradition about Abraham's call, see the intertestamental Jewish books Sir. 44:19–21 and Jub. 12:14–17. For the biblical portrait, see Gen. 11:31–12:3; Josh. 24:2–3.

6. You can flip to Jer. 34:18 to see a reference to the same ceremony.

7. It was evil because he violated Deut. 25:5–10, which says that a brother must raise up a child for his widowed sister-in-law.

CHAPTER 4

1. M. Stol, "Private Life in Ancient Mesopotamia," in *Civilizations of the Ancient Near East*, ed. Jack M. Sasson, vol. 3 (New York: Scribner, 1995), 486.

2. Gen. 41:37–57.

3. Exod. 1:8.

4. Ezek. 20:7–8.

5. The ESV says "lost" instead of "ruined," but the latter term more effectively translates the Hebrew word.

6. The Hebrew phrase behind the phrase "rose up to play" in Exod. 32:6 refers to sexual play (cf. Gen. 26:6–11; 39:6–20); see John I. Durham, *Exodus*, vol. 3 of Word Biblical Commentary (Waco, TX: Word, 1987), 422.

7. See also Num. 8:26; 18:5–6.

CHAPTER 5

1. Matt. 1:5.

2. Judg. 3:17–23; 4:18–21.

3. Judg. 8:23.

4. Although Samson was a moral train wreck, Judg. 14:3–4 says that God was able to work through Samson's sin and carry out His plan. This doesn't mean that God approves of Samson's sin. It only shows that God has the sovereign ability to hijack evil to accomplish His will (cf. Gen. 50:20; Rom. 8:28–30).

5. Judg. 8:30.

CHAPTER 6

1. See Jer. 3 and Ezek. 16 among others.

2. "Carol" is a composite real-life example gleaned from a weekend I spent on the streets of Springfield, seeking to understand what it was like to live homeless. This "poverty weekend" is a requirement for a class on urban ministry at Cedarville University, where I used to teach. I met many people that weekend—prostitutes, homeless persons, and former gangbangers—whose stories have contributed to "Carol."

3. Daniel I. Block, *The Book of Ezekiel Chapters 1–24* (Grand Rapids, MI: Eerdmans, 1997), 467.

4. Some translations say "harlot" or "prostitute" rather than "whore" or "whoredom." But despite the offensiveness of the term, the English word *whore* is the best translation of the Hebrew phrase *eshet zenonim* (literally "woman of fornications"). Harlots were women who had sex with multiple men either as a means of survival or as a means of religious devotion to pagan gods. Harlots rarely performed their services to satisfy some sexual craving, as Carol herself affirmed. But whores did, and that's where the difference lies. Hosea was commanded to marry a woman who had an addiction to sex, not one who was a victim of an evil society.

CHAPTER 7

1. Cate Lineberry, "Tattoos: The Ancient and Mysterious History," Smithsonianmag.com, January 1, 2007, www.smithsonianmag.com/ history-archaeology/tattoo.html.

2. Jer. 13:23; 2:24; Ezek. 37:1–14.

3. The phrase "lifts Himself up" comes from the Amplified Bible. This is a better translation than the more ambiguous reading of the ESV, which says "exalts himself."

4. T. Suzanne Eller, "Cutting Edge," *Today's Christian Woman*, January 2006, www.todayschristianwoman.com/articles/2006/january/11.38. html.

5. Shana Schutte, "Conquering Cutting and Other Forms of Self-Injury," Focus on the Family, 2007, www.focusonthefamily.com/lifechallenges/ abuse_and_addiction/conquering_cutting_and_other_forms_of_ selfinjury.aspx.

6. Eller, "Cutting Edge."

7. Kirsten Lamb, "Starving Yourself for Love," *Relevant*, July 9, 2010, www. relevantmagazine.com/life/whole-life/features/22198-starving-yourself-for -love.

8. Lamb, "Starving Yourself for Love."

9. Walt Mueller, "The Sad Reality of Sexual Abuse," Center for Parent/ Youth Understanding, Summer 2009, https://www.cpyu.org/Page. aspx?id=417792. According to this article, one out of every three girls and one out of every five boys have been sexually abused by the time they reach sixteen years old.

10. "Depression," Cedarville University, https://www.cedarville.edu/ Offices/Counseling-Services/Resources/Depression/aspx.

11. Gabrielle Devinish, "Study: Suicide No. 1 Cause of Death Among College Students," *The Christian Post*, November 3, 2011, www.christianpost.com/ news/study-suicide-no-1-cause-of-death-among-college-students-60444/.

CHAPTER 8

1. Technically, Joseph was betrothed to Mary, not engaged to her. My use of the word *fiancée* is meant to modernize the ancient story. Betrothal meant that Joseph and Mary were legally bound in marriage; hence the ESV's use of "wife" in Matt. 1:20, 24. However, couples were not allowed to engage in sexual activity during the betrothal period, and therefore Mary's pregnancy would have been considered fornication by her onlookers.

2. See, for instance, the use of *kataluma* in Luke 22:11. Most scholars believe that *kataluma* refers to a spare room, or perhaps the only room in a one-room house, rather than a commercial inn. See John Nolland, *Luke 1–9:20*, vol. 35a of Word Biblical Commentary (Waco, TX: Word, 1989), 105–6.

3. Matt. 2:1–12; Mark 1:24; 5:7–10.

CHAPTER 9

1. John 13:6–11.

2. Mark 14:37–38.

3. Mary Magdalene is mentioned in eight passages in the New Testament and is commonly placed first when listed with other women (Matt. 27:56, 61; 28:1; Mark 15:40, 47; 16:1; Luke 24:10). In none of these passages is she called a prostitute. This tradition comes from associating Mary with the "sinful woman" of Luke 7, but Luke never says that this unnamed woman is Mary.

CHAPTER 10

1. "Amish School Shooting," *Wikipedia*, accessed July 31, 2013, http://en.wikipedia.org/wiki/Amish_school_shooting.

2. "Amish School Shooting."

3. The Roman statesman Cicero called it "the most cruel and disgusting penalty" (*Verrem* 2:5.165) and "the most extreme penalty" (*Verrem* 2:5.168).

4. Josephus, *War 7*. 203.

5. See Heb. 12:1–2; 1 Pet. 2:21–24.

6. John 19:30.

7. Tullian Tchividjian, "Too Good to Be True," The Gospel Coalition Blog, May 2011, http://thegospelcoalition.org/blogs/tullian/2011/05/24/too-good-to-be-true/.

EPILOGUE

1. John M. G. Barclay, "'By the Grace of God I Am What I Am': Grace and Agency in Philo and Paul," in *Divine and Human Agency in Paul and His Cultural Environment*, ed. John M. G. Barclay and Simon Gathercole (New York: T & T Clark, 2006), 140–57 (156n39).

2. Barclay, "Introduction," in *Divine and Human Agency*, 7.